Well Groomed

Well Groomed

**A Wedding Planner
for What's-His-Name
(and His Bride)**

PETER SCOTT

BLOOMSBURY

Published by Bloomsbury Publishing, New York and London
Distributed to the trade by Holtzbrinck Publishers

All papers used by Bloomsbury Publishing are natural, recyclable
products made from wood grown in well-managed forests. The
manufacturing processes conform to the environmental regula-
tions of the country of origin.

Library of Congress Cataloging-in-Publication Data

Scott, Peter, 1976–
    Well groomed : a wedding planner for what's-his-name (and
his bride) / Peter Scott.—1st U.S. ed. 2006.
        p.   cm.
    Includes bibliographical references and index.
    ISBN-13: 978-1-59691-069-0 (hardcover : alk. paper)
    ISBN-10: 1-59691-069-0 (hardcover : alk. paper)
    1. Weddings—Planning.   2. Weddings—Humor.   3.
Bridegrooms.   I. Title.

HQ745.S36   2006
395.2'2—dc22
2005017991

First U.S. Edition 2006

10 9 8 7 6 5 4 3 2 1

Typeset by Westchester Book Group

Printed in the United States of America
by Quebecor World Fairfield

Contents

for my wife, Emily

(obviously)

Introduction

Planning a wedding reminded me a lot of the first time I ever went skiing. Beforehand, I was excited, a bit nervous, and knew that I needed to buy some expensive, new clothes. Later, after everything was over and done with, I was exhausted, oddly hungry for a cheeseburger, and in desperate need of a trip to Hawaii. The real surprise for me, though, came in between the beginning and the end of both events. On those occasions, there were many moments where I found myself totally confused and saying, "My God! I had no idea it would be this complicated!"

I don't mean to suggest for a second that being engaged isn't completely wonderful. It is. In fact, here's a secret that surprises a lot of women: Men really enjoy being engaged. Why? First and foremost, we're in love. And if the cost of being in love is forty-two trips to the florist over the next six months, so be it. It's a small price to pay.

The second reason men enjoy being engaged is that in accepting our engagement ring, the woman we love has agreed to let us look at her boobs for the next seventy-five years. This makes us feel very secure and happy. I've heard some women express concern that their husbands may not be as attracted to them as they grow older. Nonsense. A man's desire to look at his wife's boobs will never be satiated.

But even with the excitement of being in love (and the boob-viewing potential that came with it), there were many moments in the engagement process for which I felt totally unprepared. I kept wishing there were a tribal elder in my village who could sit me down and tell me, "Kid, just so you know, here's what your engagement is going to be like." But since I live in the village of Los Angeles, the tribal elders are also marrying women in their late twenties, so they're learning right along with me.

Something needed to be done.

What This Book Is Not

I went to the bookstore and quickly discovered that books for the bride outnumber books for the groom by a ratio of about 86,952 to 1. Moreover, the wedding books for men were all step-by-step manuals on how to be a good groom. And I think how-to books are rather silly. A doctor doesn't need a how-to book in order to remove someone's tonsils. If he does, you should think of him less as a doctor and more as a dude with a knife.

More to the point, every engagement is different and carries with it a unique set of responsibilities for each groom.

Okay. That's a lie. The truth is you don't need a whole book to explain how to be a good groom, because for 97 percent of us it can be summed up in two easy steps:

Golden Groom Rules

1. Have an opinion on everything.

2. Immediately concede that opinion when it's made clear that it's wrong (usually 2.6 nanoseconds after it's been expressed).

Consider the following example:

BRIDE: Babe, what font do you think we should use on our save-the-date cards: Times New Roman or Palatino?

GROOM: Palatino.

BRIDE: I prefer Times New Roman.

GROOM: Me too!

[*Bride kisses groom.*]

BRIDE: My mom thinks we should use Helvetica.

GROOM: Darling, I love your mother, and while we don't want to hurt her feelings, if there is a difference of opinion, I think you should always get what *you* want.

[*Bride makes love to groom.*]

How to Use This Book

Now that you know how to be a good groom (wasn't that easy?), the goal of this book is to help you be a *knowledgeable* groom. Why is this important? Because you will care a surprising amount about your wedding details. Not every guy will care the same amount, mind you, but every guy will care more than he personally expected. Planning to have no involvement? Wait until it's time to select the booze. Planning to be involved just a little bit? Trust me, after meeting with seven photographers, eleven bands, and twenty-nine caterers, you'll feel *very* involved. Planning to be the groom of the year? Then be prepared to wake up in a cold sweat at night and yell, "Did we block off enough hotel rooms?!"

Your wedding is a big event and you won't want to watch from the sidelines. Think of the engagement process as a long road trip that you and your bride are taking together. In the history of road trips, no guy has ever said, "Honey, you drive the car, and I'll just sit here quietly and look out the window without any interest in how fast you're going or which route we're taking."

At each stage of my own engagement, I found myself asking a series of questions that I never dreamed I'd be pondering. Each chapter of this book will answer one of these questions, beginning with those you'll ask moments after getting engaged and ending with the ones that will still be dancing around in your head as you say, "I do."

In the end, I hope that having the answers to these questions means your engagement will be free of the stress and confusion that typically surround wedding planning. Or, at the very least, you can laugh at the stress and confusion when they do occur, because laughter is the best medicine...unless you have dry skin, in which case I'd probably recommend moisturizer and some vitamin E instead of laughter.

Knock Her Socks Off

At the end of each chapter I've included this little section to help you, the groom, show off all the knowledge you've just gained. Consider it an insider's tip—a relevant word to add to your vocabulary, a cost-saving technique, a handy Web site— with which to impress your lady. Chances are she's already well aware of whatever you're telling her. Moreover, you'll probably find yourself accidentally using the new vocabulary incorrectly (like how I always say *coffee table* when I mean *side table*, which, in some circles, is an error more heinous than manslaughter). Nonetheless, you'll be richly rewarded for your effort.

And if you're worried that these wedding tips don't feel macho enough, you should know ahead of time that when you're engaged, your competitive juices will suddenly change from "Dude, how much can you bench-press?" to "You don't know the first thing about videographers, do you, punk?"

For the Bride

Ladies, let me first congratulate you on your recent engagement. In each chapter I have also included this section especially for you, since, as you know, it is unwise to talk about the engagement without including the bride. This book is meant to be a guide for you as well as your groom. Even those of you who have been thinking about your wedding since you were zygotes will nevertheless find that there are twists and turns in the planning stage that you didn't expect. This book will give you some additional information to complement the knowledge you have already gained over the years, because, in the words of G.I. Joe, "knowing is half the battle" (the other half of the battle, by the way, is your parents).

This section will also attempt to explain why your man has so many questions about the wedding planning, most of which must seem as moronic as asking: Is peanut butter a country and Italy a sandwich spread, or is it the other way around?

Just remember that we're usually asking these questions because we love you and because we want to learn more. Incidentally, you ask *us* dumb questions, too—not about weddings, but about other things. Questions like: "Are you sure you know what you're doing?" and "Want to try some of my tofu?"

So good luck, happy planning, and, just so you know, here's what it's going to be like.

1

How Can a Magazine Cost $12.95 and Not Have Pictures of Naked People in It?

An Introduction to Bridal Magazines

Immediately after you become engaged, and in some cases as you are putting the ring on her finger, your brand-new fiancée will celebrate the commitment you have just made to her by leaving you alone at home while she goes off to buy bridal magazines. This isn't to suggest that she doesn't already own several bridal magazines. She does. But she's hidden them, just like you've hidden your porn. Now that she's officially engaged, though, it's time for a new crop of magazines that can be proudly displayed in public. (Your porn, however, should still remain hidden.)

Upon arriving at her local newsstand, your fiancée will be met by several of her closest female friends. These friends have not been called—they have been summoned to this particular location by supernatural powers, just like all those people who drove to Iowa to watch dead guys play baseball in the movie *Field of Dreams*.

The first thing her friends will do is look at her engagement ring and discuss how much they love it. Or rather they will say how much they love it but will really be speaking in secret girl code.

What Women Say About the Engagement Ring	What They Really Mean
It's very unique!	I have the same one.
I've seen that ring at the jewelry store and admired it!	I hate my own ring.
He must have spent a fortune on that thing!	He got ripped off.
That's a big stone!	It's fake.
It looks just like my mother's engagement ring.	It sucks.
I think it's wonderful that he didn't bow to societal pressure and buy you a diamond.	He sucks.

After these pleasantries are exchanged, your new bride-to-be and her best friends will proceed to buy every bridal magazine in the store, for a total cost of $409.83. Even if your bride isn't particularly interested in bridal magazines, this is her one big chance to buy them and she feels obliged to do so. Not getting them would be like going all the way to Egypt and then skipping the pyramids because you decide it's too hot outside.

As I alluded to earlier, the best way to understand why your fiancée is spending large amounts of money on bridal magazines is to think of them as porn for the engaged woman.

Similarities Between Bridal Magazines and Porn Magazines

1. Both contain lots of pictures of women in outfits they don't normally wear.

2. There are seemingly hundreds of different magazines in both genres, each of which contains exactly the same thing. This fact, however, does not deter you from buying multiple publications.

3. Each gender justifies the purchase as "educational."

4. The ads in each magazine cause you to say, "Seriously—who would ever buy that?"

5. In a pinch, back issues can still be effective.

When your fiancée returns home with her stack of magazines, she will begin flipping through them at breakneck speed. This is not an entirely unfortunate occurrence, however. While she is looking through the magazines, you will be free to slip unnoticed into another room and watch the James Bond marathon that will inevitably be playing on some guy-oriented cable channel. Good times!

The Pandora's Box

Eventually, the magazines will begin to play mind games with you. There you are, alone in the living room, with a thirteen-dollar magazine calling to you from the coffee table. "Look inside me," it whispers softly. "No one will know. It can just be our little secret." You block out the siren's call, but your curiosity slowly starts to get the better of you. You begin to have crazy thoughts: There must be something magical inside that's really worth $12.95! A treasure map! FBI secrets! Anything having to do with Catherine Zeta-Jones! Finally, with the furor of a caffeine addict reaching for that first cup of joe in the morning, you grab the magazine and open it up.

Sadly you discover that it contains no magic formula for turning your office chair into a BMW. What's actually there is far more confusing.

What's Inside Bridal Magazines	Why It's There
74,531 pictures of wedding dresses.	For the one-in-a-trillion chance that your bride was unaware she needed a dress.
A photographic essay of a recent wedding in the Hamptons/Nantucket/Napa Valley.	Subliminal marketing message: People who spend lots of money are happy and pretty.
Pictures of supermodels wearing twenty-five-carat diamond rings.	To create conflict.

What's Inside Bridal Magazines	Why It's There
A list of tips on how to create the most perfect wedding ever!	To remind your bride that the perfect wedding has nothing to do with her feelings toward the groom and everything to do with napkin rings.
Two articles, each of which is less than a half page long.	No time to stop and read. There're still thirty-four other magazines to get through!
A preview of next month's issue, which seems as though it will contain the exact same information as this issue.	Wedding planning is stressful, so your bride can count on the security of her bridal magazines delivering the same information month after month.

The End, Not the Beginning

As strange as the information in bridal magazines appears to be, it is also, shockingly, irrelevant.

Huh? That's right. Brides don't actually need any of the information in the magazines because of the following fact of life:

Fact of Life

*Putting a ring on a woman's finger represents the end
of the wedding planning, not the beginning*

Your bride has likely been planning her wedding since long before you entered the scene. Obviously, every woman is different. Some (Martha Stewart) have spent more time thinking about wedding details than others (Britney Spears). But they've all thought about it. This is understandably difficult for a lot of guys to comprehend, because the only thing we've been planning since we were very young was to try to have a ménage à trois before we die. And in getting engaged, we've all but conceded defeat.

Your fiancée, by contrast, is now only a few steps from victory. When you give her the ring, you have unknowingly activated the Wedding Launch Sequence.

Wedding Launch Sequence

1. Bride calls her mother on the secure line.

2. Bride's mother smashes emergency pane of glass with her elbow and removes message authenticator.

3. Bride relays encrypted code to her mother. Mother authenticates message.

4. Brief silence.

5. Bride's mom screams and jumps up and down. Bride recounts details of the marriage proposal a minimum of fourteen times.

6. Bride's mother composes herself and gives inspirational speech that would make George Patton cry: "You've been trained for this moment! You know what to do!"

7. The process is repeated with bride's sisters, grandmothers, aunts, female cousins, college roommates, and, in a perfect world, Oprah.

8. Weeks later, someone tells bride's dad what's going on.

It goes without saying, I think, that there is no abort code for the Wedding Launch Sequence.

The bridal magazines exist merely to tweak the details of a project that's been decades in the making. It's like when a ship's captain makes minor changes to his route while at sea so he can avoid rough water and storms. What the captain does *not* do is set sail without a charted course and then turn to the first mate and say, "Do you know where the hell we're going?" Thus, it's a good thing that your fiancée has spent some time thinking about the wedding planning, because (a) you haven't and (b) you don't want your "marriage ship" to be steered into an iceberg. Unless, of course, you want your wedding to become the top-grossing movie of all time.

The Eternal Life of Bridal Magazines

What happens to bridal magazines after the wedding? There are a variety of answers to this question, although none of them involves the magazines actually getting thrown away.

MEMORY LANE

Bridal magazines can serve as a second wedding album for your bride. Years later she can flip through them, remember the magic of the wedding weekend, and possibly go buy another dress.

LEADING AUTHORITY

Imagine going to the Louvre and talking about art with your friends. Now imagine the same scenario, only this time you're Claude Monet. You get the idea: Suddenly, you're the badass—assuming your friends actually know who Claude Monet is. Similarly, your bride has just planned a wedding, so when she flips through her bridal magazines, she's the badass. She can become a wedding Buddha for her single friends, and the magazines are her teachings. Incidentally, your friends may also start calling you Buddha after the wedding, but that's because you've put on weight.

PASSING THE TIME

Bridal magazines can be used as a relaxing study break for your wife. On a Saturday afternoon, she'll kick off her shoes, make a nice hot cup of tea, and casually flip through an old copy of *Modern Bride*. Before you dismiss her as crazy for looking at something she's already seen a hundred times, just remember that you watch ESPN Classic.

OFFSPRING TORTURE

Your bride also saves the magazines in case the two of you ever give birth to a baby girl. Your bride thinks that it would be really cool to someday show your daughter the bridal magazines. Your teenage daughter, in turn, will think it would be really cool if you and your wife would be quiet and die.

But the biggest reason the bridal magazines stick around is because of one final similarity to pornography.

THE PORN MAGAZINE LOGIC

It's simple dollars and cents. Your bride has spent $12.95 on this puppy, so she's reluctant to toss it out. A couple of months down the road, the magazine may even make its way into a trash can, only to be rescued the following morning amid a what-was-I-thinking inner monologue. The good news is that you, the groom, can now feel less guilty about the porn magazines that you meant to throw away before the wedding, but "accidentally" kept around for much the same reason.

Thus, bridal magazines litter your home for the next several decades. With time, they develop other uses, such as leveling the uneven leg on the kitchen table or being the weapon of choice to kill mosquitoes. But try to slip an issue into the recycling bin and it will reappear magically in the living room the next day with a Post-it note that reads "Nice try."

Knock Her Socks Off

When it comes to bridal magazines, the only name you really need to know is Martha Stewart. Yes, Martha has had some legal problems, but this only seems to have strengthened most women's resolve to read her bridal magazines, as though Martha went to jail to protect the integrity of the modern wedding.

You need not have a copy of *Martha Stewart Weddings* waiting for your fiancée when you pop the question, since that's sort of weird. But if you can make Martha's magazine the one item on your coffee table that you *don't* spill salsa on, you'll be exhibiting an unexpected level of sophistication (that lasts until you spill salsa on your bride's white sofa).

For the Bride

Ladies, it's important to remind your man that you are looking through these bridal magazines for his benefit— you're getting ideas that will enable you to create a wonderful wedding for the two of you. Use this rationale even if it isn't true, because it sounds good and we're likely to believe it.

Also remember that we've probably just spent a lot of moolah on an engagement ring so we're feeling unusually frugal. Any complaints about the cost of the bridal magazines shouldn't be taken personally—we're just trying to figure out if we can go the next several decades without paying for luxuries like heat and shampoo.

And if all else fails, you can just assure your man that he'll forget about how expensive the magazines are when he learns what the flowers are going to cost.

2

Why Is Mussolini Planning Our Wedding?

Choosing a Wedding Planner

Not everyone wants or needs a wedding planner. For those who do, you must choose the right type of planner for your event. If you pick the wrong one, you will shrivel up and die. I'm not exaggerating.

The right planner for the two of you depends on your personality type.

Type of Planner	Why the Planner Acts Like This	Who Should Hire This Planner
The Dictator	Outraged that she is still single.	People who like being told that if they stand in the wrong place during the wedding ceremony, they'll be dealt with accordingly.

Type of Planner	Why the Planner Acts Like This	Who Should Hire This Planner
The Cheerleader	Her wedding was the happiest day of her life.	People who generally know what they are doing but want to be reminded to "be ag-gressive, b-e aggressive. B-E A-G-G-R-E-S-S-I-V-E!"
The Wisecracking Gay Guy	He's a wisecracking gay guy.	People who like wisecracking gay guys.
The Middle-Aged Italian Mother	"Since my own children won't get married, I had to participate in wed-dings somehow!"	People who want to hear stories about her children (and why they're not married).
The Family Friend	Looking for work after failed dotcom career.	Fellow failed-dotcom employees.
Jennifer Lopez	Desire to increase box-office power with successful romantic comedy.	Matthew McConaughey

This chart is actually provided only as a courtesy, be-cause you will ultimately wind up with The Dictator wed-ding planner regardless of your personality type. The reason this happens is that your fiancée will have attended other weddings in the past twelve months where disaster struck: The invitations had the wrong time printed on them; the band didn't show; the groom turned out to be a killer robot. Even though all these weddings concluded with the bride and groom being happily married (well, except for the one where the band didn't show), your fiancée is still spooked. She swears that such mishaps will not occur at her own wedding. Enter Mussolini.

The Regime Begins

The Dictator planner has staged a successful coup d'état in the planning of your wedding and taken control. You and your bride soon notice that your wedding preparations begin to unfold in a different manner from those of your friends who still live in a free-and-open republic.

Wedding-Planning Detail	A Couple with a Normal Wedding Planner Does This . . .	A Couple with No Wedding Planner Does This . . .	A Couple with The Dictator Does This . . .
Selection of Dinner Entrée	at a time convenient for the bride's family.	the day of the wedding.	in total secrecy, under the cover of darkness.
Organizing Guests' Addresses Using Microsoft Excel	three months before the wedding.	three months after the wedding.	at gunpoint.
Monogramming Your Dinner Napkins	with the help of a professional seamstress.	with a black Magic Marker.	with a branding iron that is tested on the groom's flesh.

Wedding-Planning Detail	A Couple with a Normal Wedding Planner Does This . . .	A Couple with No Wedding Planner Does This . . .	A Couple with The Dictator Does This . . .
Writing Thank-You Notes for Wedding Gifts	within a week of receiving the gift.	um . . . probably never.	before they even get the gift, because "you must anticipate the other party's movements if you want victory!"
The Ceremony Rehearsal	the night before the wedding.	what rehearsal?	every evening until we get it right!
Invasion of France	only if France declares war on us first.	only if someone else is paying for it.	at 0600 hours.

Of course, neither you nor your bride thinks anything out of the ordinary is happening. The other people are the crazy ones, not you guys! You're efficient! You're getting stuff done! The planner is great! Which is why, several months after the wedding, you get arrested for robbing a liquor store with the wedding planner and the Symbionese Liberation Army.

The Perks

Despite the fact you and your bride are forced to jog twenty miles at dawn (and the loser must wash the latrine), there are nevertheless many perks to having The Dictator as your wedding planner.

DEALS WITH THE VENDORS

A good planner has probably worked with your florist, photographer, and caterer before and should be able to negotiate a fair price for you with these vendors. It's not clear whether The Dictator gets these good deals through personal relationships or through a series of Amnesty International–banned torture tactics, but that's not really your concern. You're just saving money!

RUNS PARENTAL INTERFERENCE

Even the most wonderful parents can, on occasion, drive you crazy during the wedding planning. A planner can run interference by answering a lot of your parents' questions and addressing their concerns and needs. The Dictator will also order your parents to do push-ups if they continually misbehave.

BUDGETS YOUR TIME

A planner knows how long it takes to get each activity done, which helps to ensure that your guests don't receive their wedding invitations while you're on your honeymoon. And if your guests don't RSVP by the date specified? Pity them.

LENDS A HELPING HAND

You may hate an army general in basic training, but you're thrilled to have him beside you on the battlefield. So when your head starts to spin from licking envelopes, The Dictator rolls up her sleeves and dives in. When you ask if she minds the taste of glue, she tells you that she once fell into enemy hands and had to eat glue for three days straight...so this is nothing!

THE UNFORESEEN

By far the biggest perk of having The Dictator in your corner is her ability to deal with the unexpected. Videographer trying to rip you off at the last minute? No need to panic or sweat. "Let me just refer you to my planner," you say with a wicked grin. "Oh, and by the way," you add to the now visibly concerned videographer, "this would be a good time to decide if you want your ashes placed in an urn or scattered to the wind."

Wedding Planner Encroachment

Now that the planner has proven she is both useful and able to elude the authorities in the case of the incident with the videographer, everyone suddenly wants in on the action. It takes only a matter of hours until the planner is besieged with requests that clearly fall outside her realm of responsibility.

Appropriate Use of Planner	Inappropriate Use of Planner
Your brother-in-law asking the planner if she knows a good babysitter for his three-year-old daughter.	Your brother-in-law asking the planner to keep an eye on his three-year-old daughter all weekend so he can go off and get plastered.

Appropriate Use of Planner	Inappropriate Use of Planner
Bride's grandfather asking the planner to recommend a moderately priced hotel.	Bride's grandfather asking the planner to listen to a mono-logue about an infection he has in his gallbladder.
Bride's sister asking the planner for help because her bridesmaid's dress is the wrong size.	Bride's sister asking the planner for help because this is not her wedding and no one's paying attention to her.
Best man asking the planner what time she thinks the reception will end.	Best man asking the planner what time she gets off work.

Your first reaction is that you and your bride should protect the planner from these crazy people who have bizarre and inappropriate requests. You begin thinking of the planner as a European sports car—she's amazing, she's incredible, and she's probably going to break down at any minute. In which case, you're wondering why you're letting all these other people drive your fancy car.

But then you realize that the planner and a European sports car have a few key differences. First, your planner will not help you get chicks. Second, and more important, the planner is more than capable of solving her own problems. This should be painfully obvious to you by now (see: videographer, disappearance of). Give the planner the green light to deal with the problem as she sees fit. Then sit back and watch as the people bugging the planner go away. Forever.

Planner Withdrawal

During the past few months leading up to the wedding, you and the planner have worked long hours, shed some tears, and violated some laws of the Geneva Convention. Many couples are therefore surprised to discover that they miss their planner very much in the months following the wedding.

For starters, you yearn for the organizational skills that the planner brought to your life. You will find yourself staring at the jumble of frozen food in your freezer and saying things like, "The planner would never have stood for this mess," even though the fridge was a mess the whole time you were planning the wedding and the planner didn't care.

Additionally, the planner is forever associated with an exciting and memorable time in your lives. Upon returning from the honeymoon, you and your bride get jealous as soon as you realize that the planner is not only gone but also off working on another couple's wedding. It's like when an ex-lover dumps you and has sex with someone else right away. So you wind up calling the planner at two in the morning and begging her to tell you how great it was when she was with you guys.

Most surprisingly, though, you sort of miss having someone tell you what you're doing wrong. There's probably some clinical name for this psychological phenomenon, but I like calling it The Reason You Eventually Have Children.

Knock Her Socks Off

Insist that the wedding planner charge you a flat rate, rather than a commission on the overall wedding budget, which many planners will want to do. As you can imagine, planners who work on commission have a conflict of interest that manifests itself when you ask, "What should we get all our guests as party favors?" and the planner recommends Fabergé eggs.

Once you have a planner, don't be afraid to actually use him or her. It sounds obvious, but remember that you, the groom, are more than capable of e-mailing the planner yourself if you have a question or concern. You don't always have to use your bride as an interpreter.

For the Bride

Since a lot of people do just fine without a planner, you're going to have to pull out all the stops to justify the expense. Remind your man that wedding planners save you time (and time *is* money) because they will do a lot of the work. You're going to spend a lot of money during the engagement on things that make your life more difficult (like providing free champagne during the reception for your alcoholic cousin Stu), so why not allow yourself the luxury of a wedding planner who will make your life easier?

If your groom is still not going for it, tell him he can think of the wedding planner as his personal lieutenant who's there to carry out his commands during the engagement. All guys secretly fantasize about saying things like, "Prepare my fleet of ships!" and "Tell the king that victory is near!" but rarely get the chance to use any of these phrases. We're so desperate, in fact, that we'll settle for saying things like, "Prepare my Honda for the trip to the florist!" and "Tell my mom a decision on the entrées is near!" By the way, best not to mention to your fiancé that were he to actually give a command to The Dictator she'd break his spine in three places and then eat him.

3

Why Are We Getting Married in a Barn on the Outskirts of Calgary on February 4th?

The Difficulties of Choosing a Date and Venue

Picking a date and venue will be one of those wedding-planning decisions that seem really easy at first because you and your bride will be in complete agreement about what to do. You are from Denver. She is from Washington, D.C. Now you both live in Boston. As a compromise, you decide to have the wedding on nearby Cape Cod in late September. It's a beautiful time of the year in New England, when autumn is approaching but it's not yet too cold. You can get married at sunset on the beach. Afterward, there will be a clambake and maybe dancing under the stars. You can both see it in your mind, and it looks great.

Wishful thinking. First, you learn that every boathouse, doghouse, and outhouse on Cape Cod is booked until September of 2047, unless you want to get married on a Tuesday morning at quarter to seven. However, you'll have to wrap it up by nine a.m. because Genotec Corp, a strategic Internet financial consulting medical company, begins their annual corporate retreat that day.

It also turns out that Aunt Phyllis is allergic to sand, even though this is the first time anyone in the family has heard of her condition. Aunt Phyllis insists you hold the wedding somewhere other than Cape Cod; you weren't even sure that you were inviting Aunt Phyllis.

September is also out because Joan and Philip Henderson, good friends of your parents, are spending that month traveling through Asia. You've never met Joan or Philip, but your parents wax poetic about how wonderful their son Ben's wedding was. Your parents were thrilled to be invited to Ben's wedding, and it seems rude to schedule your wedding on a date that isn't convenient for Joan and Philip.

Smelling blood in the water, every person you know chimes in with an idea as to where and when you should get married. All these people will have conspired with one another to be sure that no two people could possibly be recommending the same thing. Here's a quick list of some of the times and locations that people will suggest:

Time of Year	Location
The hottest day of the year	At sea
Christmas Eve	Seven hours away from a major airport
The day before the bar exam	A living room that is way too small for the event

Time of Year	Location
Three days from now	The same hotel we used in 1945 (Note: Hotel was torn down thirty-eight years ago and there's currently an oil refinery on the site)
Hurricane season	A bug-infested field
Wednesday	Prussia

Of course, while all this debating about the location is going on, every venue in North America begins to fill up for the next three years. And suddenly a barn on the outskirts of Calgary seems logical.

The good news is that you can refer to your barn nuptials as a "destination wedding." This sounds very exciting to your guests. Originally, the term *destination wedding* was reserved only for weddings in Hawaii or western Europe, but now, thankfully, it has been watered down to refer to any place that people don't normally go to, including wheat silos and aluminum-can recycling plants.

Narrowing the Field

Eventually you'll decide that the barn isn't exactly what you were hoping for. As you hunt for a different venue, it helps to refine your search. Many people cast too wide a net when they are hunting for locations, so it's best to consider what category of venue you are most interested in using.

RELIGIOUS VENUE

Religious venues add a certain gravitas to the ceremony. However, many people have interfaith marriages these days. You may have trouble finding a religious venue that will perform the wedding if, say, one of you is a Baptist and the other founded his or her own religion that involves body surfing and eating Chee•tos.

HOTEL

Hotels host marriages all the time, which means they know exactly what they are doing. It also means that there is another wedding taking place two to three hours after yours, so seriously, Aunt Gladys, stop giving your toast about how I fell off a tricycle when I was seven because we've got eleven minutes to cut the cake and get out of here.

RESTAURANT

Restaurants provide many of the same conveniences that hotels offer and the food tends to be a bit better. Inevitably, though, the restaurant has allowed a couple of their tables to be reserved by outside patrons, who, naturally, wind up in all your pictures.

COUNTRY CLUB

Even people who don't golf will admit that golf courses are very pretty. It's awkward, however, when a sweaty man with a nine-iron wanders into your reception and asks if he can get a BLT.

MUSEUM

A museum can be a functional, elegant, and unique place to get married and have your reception. That is, until your brother spills beer on a Van Gogh while lunging for the pigs-in-a-blanket.

PARENTS' HOUSE

The good news is that there isn't a problem with availability. The bad news is that the wedding has now infiltrated every inch of personal space in your life. So, while you're at it, maybe you can have your rehearsal dinner at your office and the morning-after brunch in your car. Is that invasive enough?

UNIQUE OR SPECIAL VENUE

You are correct in thinking that no other couple has ever had their wedding in the median strip of an interstate. You are also correct in thinking that there is a reason for that.

A CIVIL CEREMONY AT THE COUNTY CLERK'S OFFICE

Simple. Quick. Easy. Cheap. Um…remind me again why we're not doing this?

The Other Couple

No matter what venue you choose, sooner or later you'll be confronted with the nerve-racking process of putting down a nonrefundable deposit to secure that location. It sounds pretty straightforward: Make out a check for some obscene amount of money to a shady-sounding corporation. So why is booking the venue angst ridden? The answer, besides your pending bankruptcy, is that you must contend with The Other Couple.

The Other Couple is interested in reserving your venue on the same day as you. If you were introduced to The Other Couple in a normal social setting at any other time in your life, you'd probably like them. In fact, you'd probably become good friends: They're about your age; they sort of look like you; they clearly have similar tastes.

Under the current circumstances, however, such a friendship is impossible. On one of your visits to the venue, you run into The Other Couple and cleverly try to talk them out of choosing the place:

YOU: You folks thinking about getting married here?

THE OTHER COUPLE: You bet! We just love the space.

YOU: Sort of cold though, isn't it? Might be kind of drafty.

THE OTHER COUPLE: Our families are from Minnesota and Maine. They love the cold.

YOU: Yeah, but what about the noise? It sounds like a shooting range next door, huh?

THE OTHER COUPLE: It's a candy factory! They make yummy chocolates that we're going to give out as wedding favors!

[*You and your bride exchange a desperate glance.*]

YOU: The last couple that was married here got divorced!

Hopefully this ruse will work. But The Other Couple is smarter than they look. If they don't go for it, everything quickly degenerates into a mad dash to see who can get their nonrefundable deposit into the hands of the venue owner first. The winners get the venue and the losers have to start their search all over again, a task that now seems as inviting as a trip to the town landfill.

Once you've won the battle and secured the venue, the emotion you'll then feel is complete and total panic—and it's not because you've forced The Other Couple to have their wedding at a Mobil station (those assholes totally deserved it!). "Why are we panicking?" you say. "We won!" Exactly. And you're totally convinced that you picked the wrong venue. You envy The Other Couple. The world is their oyster. They can still have any venue they want. You? You're locked in with no way out.

In this respect, securing a wedding venue is similar to buying a house. The minute you sign the papers, all you really want to do is wander around and look at other locations in the neighborhood. You do this with the sick hope of confirming that you got totally ripped off for what you paid.

In the event that it appears you *didn't* get ripped off with your wedding venue, you convince yourself that your location is too good to be true. Still thinking you're acting rationally, you hire a lawyer to spring you from the deal. The Other Couple quickly takes the venue and it's back to the wedding barn for you and your bride.

Picking a Ringleader for the Circus

The final piece of the venue puzzle is selecting someone to perform the ceremony. The venue you've chosen will dictate this decision to some degree. (A synagogue, for instance, may not be totally psyched about your college roommate, Teddy "Farts" McMullen, performing the ceremony.) But there are other factors to consider as well.

Type of Officiant	Pro	Con
Religious figure	Performs wedding ceremonies all the time.	Refuses to let you walk down the aisle to "Eye of the Tiger."
Actor friend who's gotten ordained on the Internet	Can do entire ceremony in Sean Connery voice.	Will do entire ceremony in Sean Connery voice.
Judge	Dignified and non-denominational.	Every time you slip up while saying your vows, he holds you in contempt and fines you two hundred dollars.
Elvis impersonator	Very memorable.	More memorable than subsequent two-week marriage.
Family member	Knows you very well.	Guaranteed to bring up embarrassing teenage moment involving parallel parking and/or trip to the orthodontist.

Type of Officiant	Pro	Con
Former U.S. vice president Walter Mondale	Elder statesman.	Rambles on incessantly about U.S. foreign policy in the late 1970s.

Whomever you choose, make sure he or she gets to know both the bride and groom equally well. There's nothing more awkward for your guests than a forty-five-minute lovefest about the bride's life achievements, followed by the officiant turning to the groom and saying, "And Ted ... I'm sure you're great, too. But enough about the groom!"

Knock Her Socks Off

The vocabulary word for this chapter is *yield*. I don't mean *yield* as in "Maybe we could have avoided the car accident if you'd observed the yield sign." In this case, *yield* refers to how many of the wedding guests you're planning to invite are likely to come. In general, you should figure that around 80 percent will attend, although that number will be slightly higher if you are getting married at the Playboy mansion and slightly lower if you are getting married in Namibia.

You should keep the yield rate in mind when selecting a venue. If you are inviting 112 people and the place you're looking at only holds 100, you should be fine. Even if you get screwed by having everyone actually show up, you can offer a credit voucher like the airlines do when they are overbooked:

Anyone willing to give up his or her seat at Table 4 will get a hundred-dollar store credit at Bloomingdale's and a guaranteed invite to the groom's fortieth-birthday party.

For the Bride

The difficulty of selecting a venue applies equally to the bride and groom, so this part of the planning won't drive a wedge between the two of you. In fact, it signals an important change in the wedding planning where the bride and groom stop thinking that they are crazy and start thinking that everyone else is crazy.

As a pleasant result, the bride and groom feel an overwhelming sense of kinship. You both vow that you'll never act like your parents when your own children get married. This is a promise you keep until years later when Ben Henderson invites you to his son's wedding, which is inevitably fabulous, and it then seems rude to have your kid's wedding at a time that is inconvenient for Ben.

4

Do We Really Need Another Tiny Crystal Bowl?

Creating Your Gift Registry

Registering for gifts is a highlight of the engagement process. You're selecting presents that people will actually get you, which makes up for all the Christmases where you asked for a bike and got travel-size soap.

You'll probably wind up registering at a place like Crate and Barrel. At first, you may be a bit freaked out because all of the salespeople (women *and* men) look like characters from a Meg Ryan romantic comedy.

But then they give you "the gun." The gun is a portable bar-code scanning device. You wander through the store with your fiancée and when one of you sees something that you want, you aim and fire. The information is saved in the gun and then downloaded into a database. Along with the wheel and penicillin, the gun makes my list of the top three most important things that mankind has ever invented.

A man with a bar-code gun is like a hamster with one of those wheels: He's pretty much entertained for the entire day. And brides get to register for eighty-seven times the number of gifts they actually need, since adding another item gives the groom a few more seconds to pretend he's Billy the Kid. It's a win-win situation.

A word of warning: The store gets to keep the gun when you're finished. However, it seems only a matter of time until Crate and Barrel lets you register for your own bar-code scanning gun.

Where to Register

Besides registering at Crate and Barrel, which I think is now required in order to get a marriage license, you may want to sign up at a few other stores as well. Here's how that process generally works:

1. The bride says she doesn't want to register at Pottery Barn and Macy's because that's where everyone registers.

2. You open registries at various boutiques that no one has ever heard of.

3. None of your guests use these registries.

4. You close those other registries and register at Pottery Barn and Macy's.

To illustrate the matter further, let's say you decide to register at a place you love called Zelda's Clock Boutique. Because Zelda's is a small operation, they don't have an online store. They also don't have parking, and they open only when Zelda feels like it. Thus, no one will shop at Zelda's.

Instead, your guests will go into their favorite boutique and get you something they think you'll love. It's a sweet and generous sentiment, but it has a success rate similar to that of the Ford Pinto. Moreover, none of these small boutiques allows you to return items, because that would be convenient and helpful. So you wind up with a dozen clocks you're not crazy about; the one you do love, at Zelda's, has been shipped back to Switzerland because no one bought it.

You have just learned an important lesson about why you should register at large, easy-to-access stores:

Important Lesson
About the Gift Registry Process

The best gifts are the ones that can be returned.

Some people may view this lesson skeptically: "What if someone gave me a complete set of bedroom furniture that costs five thousand dollars and someone else gave me a throw blanket from my registry at Pottery Barn? Are you telling me that the throw blanket is a better gift?"

Yes. Absolutely. You can return the throw blanket to Pottery Barn and exchange it for something you don't have. Alternatively, you can take a store credit and save up for a more expensive item, like a chair, a rug, or a super-expensive candle.

In contrast, your new bedroom furniture (which doesn't fit into your bedroom) can't be returned because it was made by some craftsman in Vermont, who still can't believe that he actually sold it for five thousand dollars. After weeks of haggling, the craftsman finally offers you a refund of $250. And you take the $250, because you know you can get a couple of super-expensive candles for that amount. What are you going to do with super-expensive candles? Light them. Duh.

By the way, there is one important exception to this lesson:

Important Exception to the Important Lesson About the Gift Registry Process

Cash is always welcome.

The people who give you cash as a wedding present will be talked about wistfully for the rest of time, as though they were unicorns.

Off the Registry

Even if you avoid Zelda's Clock Boutique and register at stores with easy-to-use Web sites and locations all over the country, some people will still get you off-the-registry gifts. Usually these people are close friends or family members who know you well, so their gifts are fantastic. Great off-registry items can range from a bottle of wine to a gift certificate at one of your favorite restaurants to a present you secretly wanted but were too embarrassed to ask for (Celine Dion tickets).

Other folks, however, will not know you nearly as well but still decide to take the off-the-registry plunge.

Non-Registry Gift	Justification for Giving It
A session with a psychic	"The psychic told me I'd get you this present. And she was right!"
A puppy	"I know you're allergic, but he's soooooo cute!"
A lawn mower	"How were we supposed to know you lived in Manhattan?" (Note: You've lived in Manhattan for ten years and the wedding is at Tavern on the Green.)
Milk	"You need this to help prevent osteoporosis."
A $25 savings bond that matures in fifty years	"Now you have some money put away for when you grow up." (Value in fifty years: $26.19.)

Even if you don't love a particular gift, remember not to be catty. It's touching that your guest put the time, effort, and money into picking out something special for you and your bride. That's what it's all about. Now, on to more important issues, like finding someone to whom you can you regift that lawn mower...

Selecting the Items

At the end of the day, most people will buy presents that are on your registry because they themselves have gotten married and understand the Important Lesson About the Gift Registry Process. Knowing this, you should put some thought into the gifts you select.

FINE CHINA

This is by far the *most important* registry item. In theory you get fine china because you'll want to have it on hand in the event that the Queen of England stops by unexpectedly for tea. Since that never happens, you'll eventually just leave all the unused china to your kids, who will put it in a box in the garage. Thus, in picking which china pattern to register for, the key is to be sure it differs significantly from the set of china that you currently have in a box in the garage, courtesy of your parents.

It's also worth noting that the plates will be the last thing people get you. Gravy boat? Purchased immediately. Chinese soup spoons? Line out the door. But people deem the plates to be not exciting enough and fear that years down the road you won't remember who gave them to you. That may well be true, but they should ask themselves the following question: As the Queen of England is eating off the floor due to the absence of plates, do you want to be remembered at that moment as "the gravy-boat guy"?

Besides the china, there are several other items you'll want to be sure to include on your registry.

CRYSTAL GLASSES

While typical wineglasses are lovely, crystal wineglasses can give you lead poisoning, which therefore makes them a must-have.

HIGH-END COOKWARE

How have you gotten this far in life without owning a three-hundred-dollar frying pan?

SERVING PLATTERS

The take-out Chinese food will look magnificent on these!

VASES

The one thing you definitely don't need is more vases. So put five of them on the registry.

THREE-THOUSAND-DOLLAR LEATHER SOFA

You put this on convinced that a few of your friends will team up and buy it for you. Yeah. Sure they will.

A SET OF TWELVE-DOLLAR DRINK COASTERS THAT YOU DON'T REALLY WANT

First gift you'll get.

Over-Registration

Once the registry is filled out, you'll notice that several items appear more than once—three sets of candlesticks, five tiny crystal bowls, and, of course, eleven vases. This is a phenomenon called over-registration, and there are three reasons it occurs. First, you, the groom, misused the gun and accidentally scanned in the bar code for the same item multiple times. Your bride saw this happening but was kind enough not to say anything because it looked like you were having a lot of fun, even as you aimed the red laser into some child's eye and blinded him.

Second, your bride has intentionally over-registered on several items so that you guys can return some of the extra gifts for a store credit. You can then use this store credit to get items from your registry that you really need but no one gave you (*plates!*).

The third reason for over-registration is that you, the groom, will break many of the gifts over the years. Everything you are registering for will be out of stock within three days, so your bride knows it's best to load up while you can. Her goal is to have one perfectly preserved crystal dish when you die, so that you can leave it to your children, who can put it in a box in the garage next to the china.

Dealing with the Most Awkward Moment Ever

You've gotten the gift. You didn't love the gift. You've exchanged the gift. As you can probably sense, you and your bride are setting yourself up for the most awkward moment of all time. Inevitably, anyone whose gift you have exchanged will show up at your house and want to see the gift. As panic grips your body, you need to remember one key fact: This person can't actually remember what he gave you. He just wants to see the gift he thinks he gave you and be assured that you love it and use it. So, here's what you do:

RELATIVE: So... can I see the wedding gift I got you?

GROOM: Of course! It's right over here on the mantel.

[*Groom points to vase on the mantel.*]

RELATIVE: I got you a vase?

BRIDE: Absolutely!

[*Relative stares at the vase, unsure. Bride and groom hold their breath.*]

RELATIVE: So, do you like it?

[*Bride and groom exhale in relief.*]

BRIDE: Yes! We love it!

GROOM: It's the only vase we got! Seriously!

The relative heads home happy, and several days later you accidentally knock the vase off the mantel while watching an exciting sports moment on TV. The vase shatters into a million pieces. No worries. Should the relative return, you can merely point to something else and repeat the conversation all over again.

Knock Her Socks Off

These days, most people like to buy wedding gifts online. It's easier for them because they don't have to wander through a store trying to find what you registered for; the Web sites have everything organized in easy-to-view lists. It's also easier for you because you can add and delete gifts from the comfort of your home. Make sure that the place at which you're registering has a user-friendly Web site.

If you're registering at more than one place, there are Web sites like weddingchannel.com that can provide links to all of your various online registries. That way, you can refer your guests to one site and they can peruse all of the gift options.

For the Bride

Brides-to-be: It's important to remember that men, in general, don't like acquiring random stuff. Food and DVDs never qualify as random stuff, but most registry items do. This means that at some point in the registry process your fiancé will freak out about how much random stuff you have on the list. The best way to deal with this minimeltdown is to give your groom a few "captain's picks." Let him have a couple of six-dollar beer steins, and suddenly there will be no complaints when you add the ninth pair of pillow shams to the list. And, months later, you can simply return the beer steins when he's at the gym.

5

Why Didn't I Become a Florist?

The Surprising Cost of Your Wedding Vendors

Part One: The Flowers

The first time you visit the florist, it will be as though you've arrived in a foreign country. Not only are you ill prepared to converse in this country's language, but you're also surprised to learn that everyone else around you is apparently fluent: The planner, your bride, her mother all speak "flower." Even if your bride claims she doesn't know much about flowers, you now realize that (a) she's lying and (b) she was clearly born with some sort of inherent horticultural knowledge that you'll likely never have. It's similar to the way all men—even vegetarians—think they have some preternatural understanding of how to grill meat.

You also quickly realize that the florist is the smartest person in the entire world, and not just because she knows 294 facts about orchids. No, she is the smartest person in the world because she went into the flower business. You only wish your high school guidance counselor had told you to do the same. Being an investment banker, real estate mogul, or turn-of-the-century industrialist suddenly seems like child's play.

It's not the florist's fault, mind you, that the flowers wind up costing an amount that seems equal to the GDP of Spain; it's yours.

"My fault?!" you say, shocked. Yes. It's your fault. Because every time there has been an occasion when you needed to give flowers, you have somehow found a way to never spend more than twelve dollars. At one point in time, every man has said things like, "I'm sure she wants carnations again" or "Two roses are just as good as a dozen." We've been avoiding the truth all our lives. Meanwhile, our brides have slowly become flower addicts over the years. How strong is the addiction? Just remember: Heroin comes from flowers.

The Process

Before you meet with the florist, you'll make up a list of what you'll need from her, which probably looks something like the following:

1. Centerpieces on all the tables.

2. Bouquets for the bride and bridesmaids.

3. Boutonnieres for the groom and groomsmen.

4. Maybe some additional boutonnieres for the parents and grandparents.

A florist looks at this list in much the same way a dog looks at a single piece of kibble and thinks: If this is all there is, we're going to have a big problem. The dog shows his frustration by pooping on the rug. The florist uses a different tactic that, appropriately, smells much better. The florist takes your list and adds to it the following:

5. Bouquet of flowers to put in the ladies' room and men's room.

6. An extra bouquet of flowers to put in the men's room because some drunk dude will urinate on the first bouquet "just so I could see what would happen."

7. Additional centerpieces to replace the ones stolen by guests who leave early.

8. Additional boutonnieres for any guy in attendance who has ever made out with the bride.

9. Extra rose petals to cover the passed-out wedding guest who's lying in the corner.

10. Additional bouquet for the florist's home.

You're not sure if you need everything on the florist's revised list. Yet you don't say anything, because you know it will look amazing. Also, you don't want the florist to get upset and poop on the rug.

The florist may also try to sell you special flowers that apparently only she can get. These flowers will have names like 'Lithuanian Fire Orchid' or 'Northern Lights Lilac.'

Neither the bride nor groom will have heard of any of these special flowers. This doesn't surprise the groom, because by now he's no longer paying attention to the conversation. But the bride is alarmed. She fancies herself a bit of a flower aficionado, and so she begins talking with the florist about some of the flowers she was hoping to use. The florist is prepared for this conversation and systematically convinces the bride that all the flowers she wants are wrong.

Type of Flower	What the Bride Says	What the Florist Says
Roses	"They are classic and timeless."	"Everyone gets roses. I guess you don't want your wedding to be special."
Tulips	"All the elegance of roses and a bit more original."	"Are you getting married in Amsterdam? Didn't think so."
Lilies	"Tall and striking."	"Perfect . . . if you're going to a funeral later in the day."
Gardenias	"They smell amazing."	"It's a flower your grandmother would pick."

Your bride quickly relents and agrees at once to buy whatever the florist recommends. The truth is that all your fiancée really wanted to do was show off her flower knowledge to the florist. That's right—*she* was trying to impress *the florist.* The groom awakens from his daydream and is now aware of a bizarre fact:

Strange-but-True Rule That Brides Use When Selecting Wedding Vendors

It is more important to have the vendors like you than the other way around.

Of course, this doesn't really make any sense. The vendors are working for you. You are paying them. And yet your bride regards the vendors as the Supreme Court of Good Taste. The vendors have gone to hundreds of weddings. They have seen what works and what doesn't. And if they think your bride has good enough taste that they can work with her, it's a total and complete validation of her as a person. This is true even with the vendors the bride doesn't like and has no interest in working with.

In the end, the flowers look absolutely stunning. And you have a newfound appreciation for the beauty of an elegant bouquet—which makes it all the more awkward when Valentine's Day rolls around and you once again spend only twelve dollars.

Part Two: The Music

The florist is only the first of the Holy Trinity of wedding vendors. Next up is the music. The truth is that at this point you're already behind in this area of planning. You've wasted several precious days booking your florist. Now many of the bands you'd considered are already booked.

How is this possible? you wonder. You've only been engaged for eleven days and your wedding isn't for another two years. Well, it really doesn't matter. My guess is that wedding bands have a date planner that goes about two thousand months into the future. It's actually easier (and in some cases cheaper) to book Stevie Wonder or the Rolling Stones.

Naturally, not everyone will want a wedding band. Today, there are a plethora of music options available.

BURN YOUR OWN CDS/USE YOUR IPOD

This option is becoming increasingly popular since it's a nice way to save some money. This option also allows you total control over the songs that will be played, so that you and your bride don't have your first dance to "You've Lost That Lovin' Feelin'."

The downside to this option is that you don't have anyone to emcee the reception. This seems like it's not that big a deal, until you realize that all the guests at the wedding will think the job is available to them. Thus, rather than having one person say, "Here they are, for the first time as husband and wife..." you have six people fighting for the microphone and saying things like "Bride and groom in da house!!!!"

DJ

A DJ gives you a professional MC and an enormous library of music to choose from. On the flip side, DJs tend to be enormously sketchy people. They have to be reminded constantly to (a) show up and (b) wear clothes. Additionally, most DJs wish they were working in a club in Miami. So when you ask the DJ not to play the music at a volume that causes your grandfather's ears to bleed, he informs you that you're interfering with his artistic style.

USING A BAND THAT A FRIEND IS IN

Unless your friend is Bruce Springsteen, this is a dangerous option. Your friend won't remember where the wedding is being held, but he will remember to bring his marijuana. There is a time and place to support the music career of your friend. That time was several years ago, at a bar in the East Village.

USING A RELATIVE WHO PLAYS THE ACCORDION/BAGPIPES/CASIO KEYBOARD

Everyone will love this . . . for the first six minutes.

Many people eventually opt for hiring a band, because live music really makes a party fun. Plus, the money saved by using your iPod would probably just be spent on something silly like your child's college tuition.

The best way to select a band is to go through their manager. A wedding band management company will often have twenty to thirty bands for you to choose from. Even better, the process of selecting which band to use makes you feel like an incredibly cool record producer. While listening to a band's demo CD you get to say things like "I love the voice on that baritone—so rich and full!" You're also allowed to give the band members hip nicknames such as Honey Bones and Bread Knife, and no one will make fun of you (to your face, anyway).

After you tire of the record-producer fantasy, you'll tell the manager which of the bands you like. And no matter what you say, the manager will try to sell you on one particular band:

MANAGER: So, what did you think?

YOU: I loved Soul Explosion! They sounded great!

MANAGER: Believe me, they are great! But I think you guys would be happier with the In-Tunes.

YOU: But the In-Tunes aren't a soul band. I really want soul music.

MANAGER: The In-Tunes do soul music! Absolutely!

YOU: But on their demo CD, they only sang show tunes.

MANAGER: Everyone loves show tunes! Any of those songs from *Cats* is going to be very romantic and a big crowd pleaser.

YOU: But you just said they would do soul music.

MANAGER: Show tunes it is!

The manager is pushing the In-Tunes because Soul Explosion is already booked. In fact, Soul Explosion is booked every weekend for the next twelve years. But the manager knows that if he tells you that, you'll go to a different agency to get your music. So instead he sells you on the In-Tunes, and since the manager seems like a really cool record producer, you eagerly do whatever he says.

Part Three: The Photos

There are two schools of thought when it comes to your photographer. The first is that your wedding photos are a keepsake that you will have forever, so you should get someone good. The second school of thought says that your stepbrother Len will take pictures on a disposable camera and all you have to pay him is a carton of menthol cigarettes. In the end, you'll decide to do both, which you'll describe as a "compromise" even though what you mean is "If I have to make another wedding-related decision I'm going to pull a Thelma and Louise next time I get in my car."

The great thing about many photographers is that they will have a variety of packages you can choose from.

PACKAGE A (MOST EXPENSIVE)

- Photographer and assistant will shoot your wedding day for up to ten hours.

- You get printed proofs of all the pictures from your wedding. The proofs will come in a pink Wedding

Memories box to ensure that the emasculation of the groom is now complete.

- You also get a wedding album with up to thirty-five pictures. If you want extra pictures, they are $3,500 each.

PACKAGE B (MODERATE PRICE)

- Photographer shoots the wedding for up to eight hours but doesn't use an assistant. If the photographer misses an important event like the bride walking down the aisle, she says it's because she didn't have an assistant and then she gives you crap for not getting Package A.

- You get printed proofs of 7 percent of the pictures from your wedding. The proofs come in a Ziploc bag that may or may not be clean.

- You must pay extra for a wedding album. The photos in the album are not guaranteed to be from your wedding.

PACKAGE C (LEAST EXPENSIVE)

- Photographer will advise your stepbrother Len on how to use the disposable camera.

- The photographer sells your printed proofs on eBay.

- You are given a bunch of photos to put into an album yourself. Your bride says this will be the first thing she does when you get back from your honeymoon, although twenty-five years later you are still using the photos as drink coasters.

Does Your Photographer Have the Disease?

No matter which package you choose, you'll have to wait until the actual day of your wedding to find out if your photographer suffers from a disease called Why Aren't You Taking Any Pictures That I Actually Want?! The disease, I think, is fairly self-explanatory. You may inadvertently have wound up with a photographer who dreams of having an exhibit of her work at MoMA and thinks your wedding is the perfect vehicle.

You Want...	Photographer Gives You...
a shot of the bride and her dad dancing.	several pictures of the most random person at the wedding.
a picture of the buffet spread so you can remember the amazing feast.	a series of photos showing the health-code violations in the kitchen.
a shot of the groom with his grandfather.	a dramatic, out-of-focus shot of the bathroom door.
candid photos of your friends.	a close-up of the DJ's tattoo, which depicts a man in an electric chair.
a picture of you and your bride in front of the cake.	a shot of a waiter serving a piece of cake that fell on the floor.

You Want...	Photographer Gives You...
a wide-angle shot of the reception.	a black-and-white photo of a man lying alone in the desert, dying.

The good news is that you really only need one usable picture. This picture will become your signature photo. The signature photo is the image that best captures the wedding day, whether it's the bride and groom exchanging vows or the bride and groom dancing or the groom staring at the maid of honor's cleavage.

Whatever image you choose, you'll want to order at least a dozen prints so you can put them in picture frames and give them to everyone in your family as Christmas presents. This is a monumental turning point in your life. You can now start giving pictures of yourself as presents, even though you know that the recipients of these gifts probably don't want them. Your parents and grandparents have done this to you for years. Thus, every time they come over to visit there's a mad dash to find and display the photo they recently gave you of them on their trip to China. Well, now you're all grown up and it's time to join in on the fun. Be sure to save a framed photo of the two of you to give to your son for his fifteenth birthday when what he asked for was a computer.

The Rest of the Gang

Most people think that the florist, the band, and the photographer are the only vendors they will need. Those are the same foolish people who think their parents are serious when they say that the wedding is "all about you guys!"

Not since F.D.R. introduced the New Deal has there been a put-people-to-work program like your wedding. Here's a summary of some of the other people you can employ.

VIDEOGRAPHER

A lot like the photographer, only more intrusive. Plus, after you've spent months convincing your wedding band *not* to play show tunes, there's no greater surprise than finding out that your wedding video is set to the music of *Guys and Dolls*.

LIMO COMPANY

The bride and her parents will want to arrive at the ceremony via limo, classic car, or horse-drawn carriage. The groom and his family typically arrive via taxi, mule, or not at all. The key is to request a driver with some tact. Nothing is more annoying than when you get into the limo with your bride at the end of the night and the driver turns around and says, "You're married, huh? Well, say good-bye to your freedom, buddy."

LIGHTING DESIGNER

You probably thought that lights were included. Silly groom! Your wedding needs extra lights. "Extra" in this case refers to whatever services the lighting designer can convince your fiancée to buy. To be fair, though, after your bride has spent most of her waking hours designing the centerpieces with the florist, you can understand her desire to spotlight them. Just kidding. You can't really understand it. But maybe it will look cool.

BRIDAL SUITE

Even if you're getting married close to where you live, it can be fun to splurge on a great hotel room for the night of your wedding. Moreover, it's kind of creepy when an out-of-town, unmarried businessman reserves the bridal suite, so you will be doing the hotel a big favor.

HAIR AND MAKEUP

The groom doesn't need to concern himself with this, unless you're doing some sort of costume wedding. In which case, you won't need to concern yourself with having any friends for the rest of your life.

PRIVATE SECURITY

Now you're just blatantly spending money to feel like a celebrity. And that, of course, is money well spent.

Knock Her Socks Off

One of the best ways to guarantee that you're getting a vendor you'll love is to have already seen him or her in action. If you've been to another event that had a great band, for example, you should ask that bride and groom for the name of the group. Even if you want to be original and choose a different band, you'll still be working with a reliable music management company.

The only problem with asking other couples for recommendations is that you occasionally run into a bride who gets really offended if you don't use her vendors. It seems impossible, but some people actually think, If you don't like my videographer, that means you didn't like my wedding, which means you don't like me. Solution: Say you met with her videographer and loved him, but he was already booked.

You can also ask certain vendors for his or her opinions on some of the other people you're considering using. The wedding industry is a small world, and almost all of the vendors in a certain city will know one another. If you've booked a photographer you love, ask him or her for gossip on the florists you're considering. The odds are high that your photographer will have done a wedding with each of the florists and can let you know how it turned out.

For the Bride

Getting the proper amount of groom involvement is a tricky task when it comes to meeting with the vendors. It's important to let your groom be part of the process, even though he may embarrass himself (and you) repeatedly.

Here's a helpful analogy: You, the bride, are the lead counsel on a high-profile case and your groom is the eccentric senior partner at the law firm where you work. It's painfully obvious to everyone that you, as lead counsel, are the smart one. You know what's going on and you have a plan for victory. But the senior partner likes to come to the first meeting, say hello, shake some hands, tell an awkward, rambling story that has no relevance, and then return to his office to play solitaire on his computer. Once he's gone, he's probably not coming back and you're free to actually solve the issues at hand.

6

Shouldn't I Know at Least Some of These People?

Making Your Guest List

Most of the people who are coming to your wedding fit nicely into one of three categories:

1. Friends of your family whom you have never met before

2. Friends of your fiancée's family whom you have never met before

3. People whom no one has ever met before

You will be allowed to invite your friends, but your family will invite an even greater number of their friends. If you want to invite two co-workers, for example, then your uncle gets to invite every single one of his doctors, including his podiatrist.

I'm actually getting a bit ahead of myself here, because before you argue about the guest list for the wedding, you get to argue about the guest list for the engagement party. So there should really be a subsection of this chapter called If We Don't Like These People Enough to Invite Them to the Wedding, Why Are They Coming to the Engagement Party?

The answer is that the engagement party acts as an audition for those wedding guests who you are on the fence about inviting. There are certain family members, friends, and relatives you know you'll invite. There are others, however, for whom you need more data before you can decide if they'll fit in—that random guy from your office, your dad's college roommate, your recently paroled cousin. These people's actions at the engagement party will tell you all you need to know.

Person You're on the Fence About Inviting	What He/She Does at the Engagement Party	Verdict from You	Verdict from Your Parents
Your second cousin	Gets drunk and hits on your fiancée.	"He makes us both feel uncomfortable."	"We already told him he's coming."
Your dad's fishing buddy, Ned	Monopolizes your time by telling you a long, rambling story about a school of sturgeon.	"Dad hasn't gone fishing with this guy in years."	"We already told him he's coming."
Your mom's ex-brother-in-law	Tells you about his divorce from your aunt.	"We're not even related to him anymore."	"We already told him he's coming."

Person You're on the Fence About Inviting	What He/She Does at the Engagement Party	Verdict from You	Verdict from Your Parents
The next-door neighbor, who always calls the cops when your parents have a party that lasts past nine p.m.	Calls the cops.	"You don't even like this guy!"	"We already told him he's coming."
Your mom's therapist	Tells you more about your mom than you ever wanted to know.	"I think the therapist just violated doctor-patient privilege."	"We already told her she's coming."
The caterer at the engagement party	Serves food and drink.	"She's not our friend. We just hired her."	"We already told her she's coming."

Instead of asking, If we don't like these people enough to invite them to the wedding, why are they coming to the engagement party? the real question you need to ask is... Why did you act like some of these people weren't going to be invited when you had already invited them?

There are two possible answers to this question:

- Your parents didn't want to upset you. They understand your desire for a small wedding, but at the same time they're excited to celebrate with as many people as possible.

- Your parents have gone totally insane.

In truth, both explanations are correct. One minute your parents will be acting totally rational. They'll agree to take the Mackenzies and the Wilsons off the list because they haven't seen either of those couples since an overly competitive tennis match two years ago. But then, without warning, your parents will invite their postman (with a date!). When you ask your parents what they're doing, they'll provide nonsensical reasoning like: "He brings us our mail every day. How can we not invite him (with a date)?"

Trimming It Down

The guest list has now swelled to a number that resembles the capacity of Madison Square Garden, which means there's suddenly a serious problem to address: You're inviting many more people than your venue can hold.

Once, in a simpler time, your guest list was 125 people, so you booked a venue that holds 150. But now the final guest list is 312. You can't change venues without losing your nonrefundable deposit. The only solution is to approach your parents and ask them to trim down their list. Without fail, your parents will say the following:

What Your Parents Will Say
When You Ask Them to Trim Their Guest List

"We don't need to trim the guest list because most of our friends aren't going to come."

Your parents, mind you, have done absolutely no research to confirm whether or not that statement is true. Yet they're absolutely convinced that it won't be a problem. You almost believe them...and then you remember that day when your dad said he was absolutely certain he knew how to kayak and had to subsequently be airlifted out of the Colorado River rapids.

Then, in the least surprising moment of all time, all your parents' friends RSVP yes. You have a panic attack and call your parents, and without fail they'll say:

What Your Parents Will Say When You Tell Them That All Their Friends Are Coming

"I don't know how this happened!"

Your parents are surprised, but they aren't the least bit upset. In fact, they're flattered—everyone said yes! They feel fortunate to have such a large, loyal group of friends. You feel fortunate that your parents were somehow able to provide you with food, shelter, and education, since at the moment they seem about as reliable as a traffic report.

So while your parents bask in the glow of their popularity, you and your bride are forced to go to your friends and encourage them to have children and/or be faced with a crisis at work so that they'll be unable to attend the wedding. Everyone heeds your request, and you feel fortunate to have such a small, disloyal group of friends.

The Impossible Challenge:
The Seating Chart

Narrowing the guest list down to a number below the population of Tokyo is only the first half of the battle. Once you know who's coming, you'll then be faced with the daunting task of creating the seating chart for the wedding reception. In order to do this effectively, you will need a dossier on each of your guests that takes into account important variables like (a) which guests have had sex with each other and (b) in what decade that sex took place.

To make the dossier, take a blank piece of paper and write the wedding guest's name at the top, then divide the page into two columns. In the first column, list everyone that the guest can't sit with and in the second column list the reason why.

GRANDPA EARL

Can't Sit with	Reason
1. Grandma Gloria	Ex-wife
2. Nell Thompson	Ex-mistress
3. Al Bates	Current husband of ex-mistress
4. Great-Uncle Nigel	They haven't spoken since 1955 because Grandpa Earl thinks Great-Uncle Nigel stole his Swiss Army knife.

At the bottom of the page list any other relevant seating data.

OTHER RELEVANT DATA ON GRANDPA EARL

- Hard of hearing

- Frequent men's room visitor

- Only conversation topic is the weather

Taking all this into account, you arrive at a decision for Grandpa Earl. You'll put him at Table 9, because:

1. It's down front, close to the band, so he can be sure to hear the music.

2. It's on the left side of the ballroom, which is where the bathrooms are.

3. It's near a window, so he can closely monitor the weather and have plenty to discuss with his fellow guests.

Easy, right? Now all you have to do is repeat this process for the other 249 wedding guests. This may take a while, so in order to accomplish the task you'll need to cut out "frivolous" activities like eating meals and interacting with other humans.

Even More Decisions

Now that you've got Grandpa Earl safely tucked away, there are some follow-up decisions you'll have to make.

THE FEATURED TABLE

You will first need to determine where you and your bride will sit at the reception. Many couples opt for a sweetheart table—a table for just the two of you in the center of the room. The problem with the sweetheart table is that you and your bride will feel a bit like animals in a zoo. You sit down to have a quick bite to eat and notice that everyone in the room is staring at you, taking pictures, and poking your arm to see if you bite.

You momentarily think it would be better if you guys were sitting with other guests. But just keep in mind that some family member will be deeply offended that he isn't at the head table with you, and he'll retaliate by putting you at the kiddie table every time you come to his place for a holiday dinner. Thus, the zoo situation is really the only solution. All is not lost, however. If you want a few minutes of peace with your wife, just turn around and bite one of the fingers that are poking you. Then, much like a monkey at the zoo, you'll have a few minutes of quiet before someone shows up with a stun gun.

SOUVENIRS

Next up is deciding whether you want to put party favors at everyone's place setting. The favors tend to fall into one of two categories:

1. Chocolate

2. A novelty item that your guests will immediately throw away

Knowing this, you and your bride decide that the "favor" will be the three-course dinner (with wine) that you're buying everyone.

HOW ORIGINAL

The final decision you'll face is whether to have some sort of creative name for your tables rather than just using numbers. Actually, I'm lying, because this is not the final decision you face. There is no such thing as the final decision. Wedding-related decisions are like back hair—try as you might, you can never really get it to go away. But, for the sake of sanity, you'll have to classify some decision as the final decision, even if what you really mean is "the final decision . . . for the next seven minutes."

Anyway, back to the table numbering. Instead of having Table 1, Table 2, etc., your bride will suggest that it would be more original to name the tables after your favorite movies (the *Gone With the Wind* Table), your favorite places in the world (the Venice Table), or your favorite U.S. secretaries of state (the John Foster Dulles Table).

The advantage of doing this is that Table 103 will sound more desirable if you rename it the Paris Table. On the flip side, it could create a lot of conflict if you and your bride have different favorite movies (or different favorite secretaries of state). She wants the *Gone With the Wind* Table. You want the

9½ Weeks Table. So you quickly return to the idea of just assigning numbers to all the tables and deny to everyone that you were ever considering having the Madeleine Albright Table.

Knock Her Socks Off

For many couples, creating the guest list can be the most stressful part of the wedding planning. If you fear that your guest list is spiraling out of control, one of the best solutions is to come up with a rule that you can use in deciding which people should be included. For example, when it comes to your own friends, you can make a rule that you'll only include people who (a) you've seen socially in the last year or (b) invited you to their wedding. There are obviously going to be exceptions, but making a rule will help bring some order to your guest-list chaos.

For the Bride

Ladies, up to this point in the wedding planning, your fiancé has probably kept his cool. He's likely been a calming influence on you. Even as he learned what various aspects of the wedding were going to cost, he's tried his best to handle it with grace and class. That classy behavior ends with the guest list.

It's completely normal for your groom to start having severe emotional swings. Maybe it's the awkwardness of celebrating his wedding with a hundred people he's never met before. Maybe it's the potential fire hazard you'll be creating when you put 250 people in a room designed to hold fourteen. Or maybe he just hates licking stamps. Whatever the reason, you can expect that he'll be saying things like "Let's include all our wonderful friends and family!" one day and then, the next day, it's "What do all these vultures want from me?!"

If you need to calm him down, just start making up names of imaginary people and tell him you're taking them off the guest list: "Honey, don't worry, because I just decided that Julie Weston and Guy Davidson aren't getting invites." Your groom has never heard of Julie Weston and Guy Davidson, of course, but since he hasn't heard of most of the people on the guest list, he'll never catch on.

7

Do All These Drunk People Really Need to Be on a Sugar High, Too?

The Wedding Cake

Nothing symbolizes true love better than a twelve-hundred-dollar pastry. You must spend the money, though, because your guests will be absolutely devastated if you don't have a cake. Even your diabetic friends would rather attend a wedding with no groom than one with no dessert. So off you go to a variety of bakeries to taste cake. When you were twelve years old, this sounded like the best activity of all time ... then again, so did setting your farts on fire. What should that tell you?

The fact is that the cake tasting can be surprisingly stressful for both bride and groom. The bride is tense because she is trying to lose weight before the wedding. The cake is therefore an evil specter that looms over the event. It's like a psycho ex-lover who shows up at your birthday party—only worse, because you can't have passionate I-hate-you sex with a cake.

Meanwhile, the groom is stressed because he has to find the vocabulary to describe all the different types of cake he's eating, even though what he's thinking is: "Cake good. Me happy." It's similar to the stress the average guy feels when he has to order a bottle of wine in a nice restaurant. The selection of the wine is hard enough, but the tasting is the real kicker. Unless an animal crawls out of the bottle and starts attacking, we're not sending the wine back.

And yet, there we are, having a cake tasting, trying desperately to come up with an adjective besides "bitchin'!" The more cake you have, the more delicious it tastes and the more moronic you sound when you try to analyze it as though you were a connoisseur.

Cake Flavor	Moronic Way You Describe How It Tastes
Chocolate cake	"Oh man. This is sooooo good. It's like really, really good."
Lemon cake	"This is so lemony."
White cake with raspberries	"I can taste the raspberries. Like really taste them. And they taste good. Really, really good."
Almond cake	"If you like almonds, you're gonna love this cake."
Carrot cake	"You think carrots and you're like 'oh no, a vegetable.' But this isn't like a vegetable. It's like a dessert. A really, really, really good dessert."

Cake Flavor	Moronic Way You Describe How It Tastes
Tiramisu cake	"Whenever I go to an Italian restaurant and they have tiramisu, I always get it. And now, I'm not at an Italian restaurant, but I'm still having tiramisu. You know what I mean?"

Thankfully, whichever cake you choose will ultimately be delicious. And it's nice to finally have a wedding-related decision where you can't go wrong no matter what you choose . . . that is, until you discover you're allergic to almonds.

Inside vs. Outside

The cake's interior is only the first part of the equation. You must also decide what the outside of the cake will look like. In order to help you along, the baker (or "dessert specialist," if he's really expensive) will have a book with photos of some of the cakes he's created over the years. The cakes will range from the classic (white fondant with flowers) to the creative (cake shaped like the Empire State Building) to the bizarre (cake shaped like Cher's head).

After flipping through the book and having a grand old time, your bride will turn to a picture near the front that shows a traditional white tiered cake. She'll tell the baker that this is what she has always had in mind.

The baker frowns, as though she had just told him that she wants the cake to be made entirely of veal. The baker takes the book, turns to the picture of Cher's head, and informs you that this is the cake you want. He then uses the flavor you have picked out as some sort of odd justification: "Well, if you're going with the lemon filling, I think Cher's head is really the proper shape." This sets off a barrage of questions in your mind, most notably: How does he know what Cher's head tastes like?

The real reason the baker is pushing Cher's head is that every day he makes seventy-five tiered cakes with simple white frosting and flowers. He's never actually made any of the other cakes in his book—he cut those pictures out of magazines, hoping that someone would want something besides a tiered cake with white frosting and flowers.

Since the baker is now starting to seem crazy, you and your bride decide to check out the other cake places around town but soon discover that the alternatives aren't much better.

TYRANNICAL FRENCH BAKER

Makes the most delicious cake you've ever had, but decides you don't deserve it.

FRIEND WHO IS AN AMATEUR BAKER

Has never made a cake that can feed more than four people, but "can't see what could possibly go wrong."

THE STRESSED-OUT BAKER

You tell him you need a cake to feed a hundred and fifty people and he says, "Jesus—that's gonna have to be a really big cake!"

THE BAKER AT THE SUPERMARKET

Doesn't know how to make a wedding cake, but is pleased to let you know that the chocolate chip cookies are on sale this week (three dollars a dozen with the club card).

CRAZY OLD LADY BAKER

She's wonderful, but in the three hours you spent with her, you never actually talked about cake, just her grandchildren.

ANITA BAKER

Performing at the MGM Grand the night of your wedding.

Thankfully, the first baker you visited calls you and tells you he's realized that the Cher's head cake was a bad idea. Madonna, on the other hand . . .

During the Wedding

When the actual wedding day rolls around, you quickly discover that there are a series of bizarre traditions that surround the wedding cake.

**BIZARRE TRADITION #1: PUTTING THE CAKE ON DISPLAY
FOR THE ENTIRE NIGHT**

In a way this makes sense. The cake is expensive and beautiful—why not show it off? The reason this is a bad idea is that the entire evening soon turns into a Buster Keaton comedy where guests come perilously close to knocking the cake over throughout the night.

Even if the cake isn't knocked over, the room temperature causes it to melt and list to one side. You're forced to cut the cake eleven seconds after dinner ends. The minute the knife hits the frosting, the entire cake disintegrates into a puddle.

BIZARRE TRADITION #2: EVERYONE GATHERING AROUND WHILE YOU CUT THE CAKE

We've come to think this tradition isn't strange because it's been around for a long time. Imagine, though, that you're sitting down to dinner and about to cut your first piece of steak. Suddenly, everyone in the room gathers around to watch you. As your knife hits the filet, the photographer snaps a picture, everyone claps wildly, and the waiter immediately wheels the filet away so that he can cut the rest of it in the kitchen.

BIZARRE TRADITION #3: SMEARING FROSTING ON YOUR BRIDE'S CHEEK AS SHE EATS THE FIRST SLICE

A lot of couples decide that they don't want to observe this tradition. Not only are you both wearing the most expensive outfits you've ever owned, but the cake also costs something like thirty-two dollars a slice. Plus, you each have a mouth, which has always served as an effective receptacle for food.

Your guests, though, will not stand for civil behavior. They will demand some sort of cake-face action. The scene quickly degenerates into *The Jerry Springer Show*, with the crowd egging on the bride and groom until they get what they want. (Afterward, Jerry brings out some random chick the groom hooked up with twelve years ago, and she and the bride have a fistfight.)

BIZARRE TRADITION #4: SAVING THE CAKE FOR A YEAR

This is the strangest tradition of them all. You're supposed to freeze the top part of your cake for a year and then eat it on your first anniversary.

If it's not obvious, here's a list of some of the problems that can arise if you follow Bizarre Tradition #4.

Problems Associated with the Tradition of Freezing the Top Part of Your Cake and Eating It on Your First Anniversary

1. Your brother, who was in charge of freezing the top part of the cake at the end of the wedding, convinced himself that you'd never notice if he ate two slices.

2. Over the course of the year the cake has inadvertently come into contact with every other food in your freezer. Thus, the cake is now mingled with runaway frozen peas and a rogue piece of pepperoni from a Stouffer's pizza.

3. During a snowstorm last winter you lost power for a day and a half, so the cake looks less like the dessert from your wedding and more like *Night of the Living Dead*.

4. The cake takes a week to thaw, by which point your anniversary is over.

5. When you finally are able to eat the cake, it tastes remarkably like cake that's been in the freezer for a year.

Luckily, your baker will gladly make you a small, fresh cake for your first anniversary. That way, you can observe the tradition and enjoy a delicious cake. Just don't send your brother to pick it up.

Knock Her Socks Off

Most bakeries charge you a per-person fee for the cake. For example, if the cake costs four dollars per person, it will cost four hundred dollars for a wedding cake that feeds a hundred people, and eight hundred dollars for one that feeds two hundred people. One easy way to save money, however, is to get a smaller cake than you need and have the baker bring extra sheet cake in the same flavor. Sheet cake is cheaper (one or two dollars a slice), so if you get a wedding cake for a hundred people and sheet cake for a hundred people, you're spending only five hundred dollars instead of eight hundred. Sheet cake tastes exactly the same, and since the cake is cut up in the kitchen, no one will know the difference.

The baker may also let you mix and match flavors for no additional charge. Each tier of the cake can have a different filling. If you can't decide between two types of cake—try them both! Just remember that each guest is only going to get one piece of cake, so if you serve more than two flavors, it will be difficult (and sort of gross) for everyone to get a taste of each type.

For the Bride

Ladies, it is totally okay if you don't want your groom to smear frosting on your face during the cake cutting. *However, you must tell him in no uncertain terms not to do it.* Don't assume he knows what you're thinking. You should have already figured out by now that while your groom loves you, he isn't great at reading your mind. Remember the first Valentine's Day you spent with him? You were hoping for earrings and he was absolutely convinced that you wanted a Jessica Simpson bobblehead doll. Don't make the same mistake twice.

8

Is There Anyone Coming to the Wedding Who Isn't a Bridesmaid?

Selecting the Bridal Party

At most weddings you go to, you'll notice that there are usually the same number of bridesmaids and groomsmen. This is done to create a balanced image for the guests when they watch the ceremony. If there are too many groomsmen on one side of the room or too many bridesmaids on the other side, the bride and groom will not be the center of attention. Instead, groomsman number three is weirdly at the geographical center of the group, which means everyone is staring at him as he picks his nose and yearns for a cigarette. Not good.

With that in mind, you sit down and make up a list of the guys who you'd like to have as groomsmen. While there may be a couple of difficult choices (do I ask both my college roommates or just the one whose name I remember?), you have a pretty good idea of who you'd like to include. You have a couple of close friends and relatives who seem like obvious picks.

Your bride, in shocking contrast, has a list of at least three dozen potential bridesmaids. She's already cut the list down (the first draft had over a hundred names) and says that it is going to be very hard for her to cut it down further, because everyone who's on it is a very close friend. Incidentally, in the five years you and your fiancée have been dating, you've never heard her mention the majority of the "very close friends" on the list.

Your first reaction is to be introspective: Why don't I have more friends? Am I not as social a person as I originally thought? It's an interesting moment for you because, maybe for the first time in your life, you're on the edge of really understanding yourself. This scares you, so you quickly end that train of thought and set about finding more groomsmen—a challenging task since you're going to need more guys in the wedding party than you have friends. This means that if you meet *any* dudes before the wedding—a co-worker, a new tenant in your apartment building, your UPS delivery guy—you go into instant sales mode:

UPS DELIVERY GUY: Hey man, got a package for you. Looks like something from a bridal registry.

YOU: [*making conversation*] We're getting close to the wedding date.

UPS DELIVERY GUY: Oh yeah? When *is* the big day?

YOU: Three months.

UPS DELIVERY GUY: That's great! I had the best time at my wedding.

YOU: You should come by if you're not doing anything that day.

UPS DELIVERY GUY: [*hesitant*] Um ... thanks. I'll have to check my schedule.

YOU: You could even come early if you wanted. And maybe wear a tux. And maybe walk down the aisle with the daughter of my fiancée's boss.

Not surprisingly, you have a new UPS man the next day.

The Best Man

Once you've gotten your groomsmen in place (the FedEx guy was, luckily, more receptive to your overtures than the UPS guy), it's time to choose your best man. This is not a decision to be taken lightly. Not only is it a special honor for one of your friends or family members, but the best man also has several important responsibilities.

Important Responsibilities of the Best Man

1. Plan the bachelor party.

2. Apologize profusely when forgets to plan bachelor party.

3. Give toast during the wedding.

4. Make serious effort to stay sober at wedding until after giving the toast.

5. Apologize when all efforts to stay sober fail.

6. Generally be available to help the groom with any issues or troubles he may encounter during the wedding planning.

7. After groom explains his troubles, respond with: "I don't really know what you're talking about. Let's go to a Cubs game."

8. Apologize when unable to get Cubs tickets.

Most guys have several close friends and relatives who could fulfill these duties. The decision is a difficult one. To help narrow the field, you can use the following chart to assign a point value to each of the guys you are considering. Guys earn points by having favorable attributes for a best man.

Attribute of Best Man Candidate	Point Value	Reason
Married	+10 points	Has been in the trenches of wedding planning and lived to tell about it.
Divorced	–5 points	Has been in the trenches of wedding planning and did *not* live to tell about it.

Attribute of Best Man Candidate	Point Value	Reason
Married to a masseuse	+20 points	Only time in your life you can say, "I need an hour alone with your wife" and not get punched.
Physically strong	+7 points	Has ability to scare away those wishing to give awkward toasts at rehearsal dinner.
Compulsive gambler	+5 points	Knows his way around Vegas, which is helpful at the bachelor party.
Has young children	−3 points	Pro: Very responsible. Con: Views your wedding as a chance to catch up on much-needed sleep.
Is significantly more successful or attractive than you	−20 points	Don't want to be standing at altar while your bride looks at the best man and thinks, How come I'm not marrying that guy?
Has X-ray vision	+300 points	How cool is that?
Is a close friend	+2 points	Not nearly as cool as having X-ray vision.

Once you've tabulated the point total and determined which one of your friends has the most points, you'll call him up and ask him to be your best man—only to learn that he is already going to another wedding that same day. So you call the guy with the second most points and he tells you that he'll be at his grandmother's eightieth-birthday party that weekend. Eventually, you get down to the guy in ninth or tenth place. You call, expecting him to decline. When he accepts, you immediately perk up and say, "What luck that my first choice was available."

Your bride, meanwhile, is also having trouble picking a maid of honor. She has a larger pool of friends to choose from, and she's well aware that the maid of honor's responsibilities easily trump the best man's:

Important Responsibilities of the Maid of Honor

1. Spend a minimum of two thousand hours discussing details of the wedding with the bride.

2. Repeatedly tell bride how much she loves the china pattern on bride's registry.

3. When something goes wrong with bride's wedding plans, must be ready with amusing anecdotes about other people's wedding-planning mishaps.

4. Spend minimum of two thousand hours discussing details of bridesmaids' dresses.

5. Give toast at wedding that is less offensive than best man's toast.

6. Tell bride she looks beautiful, even if bride just changed a flat tire in the pouring rain.

7. Spend a fortune of her own money on an engagement present, a shower present, a wedding present, a dress she'll never wear again, shoes she probably won't wear again, and travel expenses.

8. The week after the wedding, spend minimum of two thousand hours discussing how everything went.

Your bride soon decides that these responsibilities are too much for one person to handle, so she's going to have two maids of honor. This, in turn, means you need a second best man. Looks like the FedEx guy is in luck!

The Bridal Shower

There is one additional responsibility faced by the maid of honor: planning the bridal shower. No other wedding-related event is as mysterious for the groom as his fiancée's bridal shower. The reason for the confusion is that (a) the groom is specifically *not* invited to the shower and (b) there's no equivalent celebration for him that could provide any insight.

So, when your bride heads off to her shower, you, the groom, are left alone to ponder what she'll be doing. Given some mental freedom, you quickly decide to abuse it. The name "bridal shower" sounds fairly sexy to you. It seems to imply that your fiancée will be given some sort of bubble bath by all her female friends. You convince yourself that this is a tradition handed down from Greek mythology. In olden times, bridesmaids, nymphs, muses, and goddesses took the bride down to the river to wash her so she would smell clean and fresh for her groom. For good measure, everyone was naked when this happened.

While you are daydreaming, your bride returns home from her shower and wonders why you are sweating. You snap out of your haze and ask your fiancée if she had fun. Since the event is now over, your bride reveals the details of the shower to you.

Highlights of the Bridal Shower

THE TEA PARTY

After all the ladies arrived at the shower, they spent at least an hour socializing over tea, cookies, and little sandwiches. The topics of conversation ranged from weddings to children and then back to weddings again.

Most guys are mystified as to why this part of the shower takes an hour to complete. Were it a bunch of guys, the tea party would last exactly four minutes, because that's how long it would take us to (a) eat all the food and (b) exhaust every topic of conversation.

OPENING THE GIFTS

This is the most awkward part of the shower. The bride opens all her gifts while everyone else stands around and tries to look excited. In fact, everyone is bored to tears because there's only so long you can stand around and look at gifts that aren't being given to you. Moreover, all the ladies at the shower have already gotten your bride an engagement present and a wedding present, and they are moments away from simply handing your fiancée an invoice for all the gifts—the only thing that's preventing them is the knowledge that they can even the score when they themselves get married.

Your bride has been to other showers and knows how boring the opening of the gifts can be. She therefore tries to open the presents as fast as she can. As a result, many of the guests assume your bride doesn't like her gifts because she isn't spending forty-five minutes praising the quality of the potholders she's just received.

In an attempt to make the gift opening slightly more exciting, there may be a theme assigned to the shower presents. When women exchange engagement gifts, they generally give champagne or flowers, and wedding gifts tend to be something substantial from the registry. The shower is thus a chance to have fun. Popular shower themes include: gifts for the kitchen, gifts for the body, or gifts that the bride already has.

The most popular theme, however, is sexy lingerie. The theory behind giving sexy lingerie is that it's a gift for the bride that the groom will no doubt appreciate. The only problem with this theory is that the sexiest piece of lingerie will come from someone surprising, like the bride's grandmother. Every time the bride puts on her revealing nightie, both she and the groom will be thinking of Grandma ... which can, um, be awkward.

FUN AND GAMES

After the gifts are opened, everyone wants to go home. The shower is for your bride, however, so who cares what everyone else thinks, feels, wants, or needs? There are still some bridal games to be played!

Although every shower has its own games, there's usually some sort of quiz for the bride about her groom. One of the bridesmaids will contact the groom ahead of time to get his answers to questions like, What was the name of your senior prom date? and What's your favorite brand of beer? and Have you ever hooked up with any of the bridesmaids? Everyone has a great time, except for the bride, who's pretty sure she didn't want to know 93 percent of the facts she just learned about her future husband.

Sometimes, the groom quiz can be combined with the gift opening—the bride can't open another present until she correctly answers a question. Combining the events keeps the guests interested in the gift-opening process. It also means that opening the gifts takes from five to seven hours because your bride didn't know that your favorite type of beer was "whatever they're selling by the gallon."

Tiny People

Once the bridesmaids and groomsmen are locked in, you'll then have to decide if you want to have a flower girl and a ring bearer as part of your ceremony. There are some important considerations to weigh.

Reasons to Have Ring Bearer and Flower Girl	Reasons *Not* to Have Ring Bearer and Flower Girl
Supercute . . .	. . . until they fall down and start screaming.
Everyone will be admiring them.	Which means they won't be admiring the bride.
The kids' parents will be absolutely thrilled.	Every other kid's parents will be pissed you didn't use their child.
What's prettier than having flower petals on the aisle?	Flower girl doesn't actually get the petals on the aisle; she squeezes the petals into little balls and throws them at people.
Babies are good luck.	Just as the kids are approaching the altar, they look up, see the groom, and then run away crying. You're telling me that's good luck?

Eventually, you decide that you don't need two emotionally unstable kids running around—that role has already been filled by the maid of honor and best man.

Knock Her Socks Off

There are logical ways to limit the size of the bridal party if you and your bride feel it is growing too large. You can just have a best man and a maid of honor. You can just have siblings. Or you can have a representative from each group of people to whom you are close—one family member, one high school friend, one college friend, and one friend from work.

Even those friends who aren't bridesmaids or groomsmen can still have special roles at your wedding. They can give a toast. They can escort an important family member down the aisle. They can even sing a song during the reception (as long as your friend is Beyoncé).

For the Bride

If your fiancé is really stressing about finding enough grooms-men to equal your number of bridesmaids, you can let him off the hook. Modern weddings do not really require you to have even numbers on both sides of the aisle. If you have more bridesmaids than groomsmen, some of the bridesmaids can just walk down the aisle unescorted. They can sit isolated and alone at the head table. Later, they can just dance by themselves. By the time you toss your bouquet, they'll be in tears. So, on second thought, screw your fiancé's feelings. If he's having trouble finding eighteen friends to be in the bridal party, do you really want to be marrying him?

9

Why Are You and Your Mom Acting Like Rival Street Gangs?

The Complicated Relationship You Have with Your Parents During the Wedding Planning

Regardless of the existing relationship between your bride-to-be and her mother, there will be conflict during the planning of the wedding. It doesn't mean that anyone is doing anything wrong. It doesn't mean that anyone is a bad person. It's just something that happens to everyone. Even if your bride and her mom are normally so close that they floss each other's teeth, at some point during the engagement they will try to strangle each other with the floss.

It's a conflict going back generations. It's Athens vs. Sparta. Man vs. beast. Valet parking vs. "Let's look for something on the street." Oftentimes the disagreement appears to have little to do with the wedding itself. While there may be feuds over the dress or the guest list, there could just as easily be a fight over the dew point, Faulkner's best novel, or the capital of Peru.

There are certain moments when the mother-daughter conflict spills out into the open; one of the most common is during an event called The Really Awkward Dinner with Your Bride and Her Parents.

The really awkward dinner with your bride and her parents starts out perfectly normal. You'll all be at a restaurant, having a lovely time. And then, in an instant, things begin to go bad. The catalyst isn't particularly obvious—your bride asks her mom to pass the butter, her mom says it's actually margarine, and then they're off to the races. Both women will head to the ladies' room in tears. Five minutes later they will return to the table acting like the closest of friends. Five minutes after that they'll return to the bathroom in tears.

The upside is that while the ladies are in the rest room, you'll have a chance to bond with your future father-in-law. This basically involves your fiancée's dad telling you his life's philosophy in under three minutes. The conversation will go something like this:

BRIDE'S DAD: Now that the ladies are gone, let me tell you the only thing you'll ever need to know about being married.

GROOM: [*concerned*] Okay.

BRIDE'S DAD: Men—we're simple. Steak. Beer. Sofa. We're all set. But women—jeez, they're complicated. They're always going to the bathroom in pairs, which I think is really weird. Do you know what I mean?

GROOM: Um … sort of.

BRIDE'S DAD: Don't ever ask if you can come to the bathroom with me.

GROOM: No, sir.

BRIDE'S DAD: Also, when you go to a sporting event, there's always a line outside the ladies' room, but not the men's room.

GROOM: I see.

BRIDE'S DAD: Women have to pee all the time. If you ever take a road trip, you're gonna have to make like five or six stops so your wife can pee. That's what marriage is like.

GROOM: Great. Thanks.

[*Groom and bride's dad eat their steaks in silence until the women return.*]

Man Bonding

Despite the overwhelming awkwardness of the let-me-tell-you-about-women-and-their-peeing-habits conversation, your future father-in-law will, remarkably, want to spend more one-on-one time with you. This is because he's always wanted a son, and while he's not necessarily crazy about you, he knows that you'll at least listen to all his stories because you're too scared not to. So off you go to do one of the following mantivities together.

THE BALLGAME

Good, old-fashioned fun…until your bride's dad starts heckling the shortstop with a profanity-laced tirade, making you wonder what he'll say to you if he doesn't like the birthday present you got him.

HUNTING

Odds of you shooting an animal are much less than the odds of your father-in-law accidentally shooting you in the foot "just so you know who's the boss."

GOLF

You let your father-in-law win, until he starts talking trash. You then make a great shot, start talking trash back to him, and he stalks away, pouting. Later, your bride yells at you for hurting her dad's feelings.

WORKING AROUND THE HOUSE

This is a nice preview of the rest of your life. At first, your father-in-law only calls you to help with major tasks like building a deck or winterizing the swimming pool. Eventually, though, he'll get lazy and ask you to come over and put a fresh roll of toilet paper in the bathroom.

POKER NIGHT WITH HIS BUDDIES

You're fairly confident you can handle yourself, until you realize the ante is five thousand dollars. When you hesitate, the bride's dad says, "Are you gonna be a pussy in front of all my friends?" Yes. Yes, you are.

SAILING

You'll get out into the open water and your bride's dad will suddenly ask you if you feel like smoking a joint. While you scramble to come up with the correct answer, the bride's dad, now stoned, starts telling you about the night your bride was conceived.

POWER LUNCH

Pretty much a total replay of the dinner you've already had together, because the bride's dad can't remember if he told you his thoughts on women going to the bathroom, so, just to be safe, he tells you again.

The Groom's Parents

If the bride's parents seem, at times, to be too emotionally involved in the planning, then your parents will provide a striking contrast. They are not necessarily easier to deal with, mind you—just different. Your folks are completely oblivious to everything that's going on. Frankly, they're pleasantly surprised to have been invited to the ceremony. In fact, your parents will be so caught up in their own affairs that they need to be reminded that they should (a) make hotel reservations and (b) attend the wedding.

The conversations between you and your own father will be strikingly different from the ones you had with your future father-in-law:

GROOM: Hey, Dad. There were a couple of wedding-planning details I wanted to discuss with you.

GROOM'S DAD: Mom just got me TiVo for my birthday, and I'm having all sorts of problems with it. How do I make it stop recording random programs?

GROOM: I'll show you next time I'm home. Anyway, we want you to give a toast at the wedding . . .

GROOM'S DAD: We're off to Virginia Beach on Wednesday! We haven't been in a couple of years, and I know your mom is really looking forward to it.

GROOM: Sounds great. Now, when you come for the wedding you may want to rent a car . . .

GROOM'S DAD: Tell me again what day you're marrying Shannon.

GROOM: June first. And her name is Sharon.

The groom's mom, meanwhile, wants desperately to plan the entire wedding, but knows that is an unrealistic goal. To cope, she decides to use the entire event as a research project for a future wedding when she is the mother of the bride (and therefore can plan the entire thing). She'll pepper the groom with questions that he obviously isn't going to know the answers to, such as Are the bridesmaids wearing their hair up?

Though your mom will be more than capable of driving

your sister up a wall when the moment is right, for now, she is the feel-good person of the year. Whatever your mom says is comforting to your bride and whatever her mom says is stressful. If both your mom and her mom see the wedding dress and your mom says, "It's interesting but not what I would have chosen," all your bride hears is "gorgeous." If her mom says, "I think it fits you perfectly. It's exactly what I always envisioned your dress would look like!" all your bride hears is "I am planning this whole wedding and there's nothing you can do about it! Ha!"

Back in the Day

There will be one important similarity between the bride's parents and the groom's parents: They will continually reference their own weddings throughout your engagement. In many instances, these comparisons are both welcome and heartfelt. The groom's parents, for example, may reminisce about how excited they were during the days before their wedding and note that the two of you seem just as enthusiastic. Alternatively, the mother of the bride may break out her wedding album, which leads to an emotional trip down memory lane for mother and daughter.

Unfortunately, both sets of parents will also draw comparisons to their own weddings that won't be the least bit helpful.

UNHELPFUL COMPARISON #1: WEDDING-BUDGET DIFFERENTIAL

At some point, the parents will note that your wedding is costing a lot more than their wedding did. Even if your mom and dad work for the Federal Reserve, they will refuse to accept inflation as the most obvious and logical reason. Your dad tells you that a wedding ring thirty years ago cost $30. You explain that the price has gone up substantially since then. Your mom responds by telling your dad that they spent only $25 on each ring, not $30. Your dad insists it was $30. They spend the rest of the day arguing.

UNHELPFUL COMPARISON #2: NEIGHBORHOOD CHANGES

Not long ago, no one ever would have dreamed of getting married on the wharves because they were in a high-crime area. Now, thanks to urban renewal, the waterfront has become a thriving center of commerce, complete with several hotels and spaces to hold events. Your parents, however, only want to tell you about a friend who was mugged on the docks twenty-five years ago:

YOUR MOM: Alice was never the same after the mugging!

YOUR DAD: Never!

UNHELPFUL COMPARISON #3: ATTIRE

Over the years Americans have become more casual in the way they dress. In 1952 you'd wear a tuxedo to buy milk. Now people wear T-shirts to presidential inaugurations. So it simply isn't important to you that every male guest at your wedding be wearing a tie. Your parents are mortified and insist that those guests can't be in any of the pictures, even though "those guests" comprise everyone in attendance besides them.

UNHELPFUL COMPARISON #4: THE RECEIVING LINE

It used to be common for the bride, the groom, and their parents to line up after the ceremony and greet all the guests as they filed into the reception. Today, many people skip the receiving line because it creates a huge logjam as people try to make their way to the cocktails. It's easier for the bride and groom and their parents to wander around during the course of the evening and greet the guests individually rather than doing it all at once. Your parents, however, may insist on having a receiving line because "it's what everyone did in our day." They won't be dissuaded, even after you point out that people also had unprotected sex and smoked cigarettes in maternity wards back then.

UNHELPFUL COMPARISON #5: YOU'RE NOT INVITING THE MAYOR?

In the small town where your parents grew up, it was unheard of to have a wedding and not invite Mayor Frank P. Wilson. Even though you are getting married in Chicago and have no connection to the mayor, your parents insist that you send him an invitation. Don't worry: He's not coming.

The Meeting of the Minds

Since both sets of parents take you on a trip down memory lane, you assume (incorrectly) that they have a lot in common. You arrange a dinner where everyone can meet. After pleasantries are exchanged, both sets of parents will make an attempt to bond with one another by saying how much they adore the bride and the groom. What should be touchingly sentimental for everyone quickly degenerates into a competition over who loves the children more.

Making matters even more awkward, your dad will soon start talking about a dowry. Your dad has never mentioned this topic to you before. You assume he's kidding since (a) this isn't the Middle Ages and (b) your dad wouldn't know what to do with a donkey if the bride's family gave him one. To your horror, though, you soon realize that your dad isn't kidding. He doesn't want a donkey (thankfully), but he's at least looking to have the father of the bride pick up the tab for dinner.

And suddenly everything makes complete sense. The tension, the fights, and the conflicts that you've been experiencing with both sets of parents have really been about one important subject: Who's paying for what. Even if you and your bride are willing and able to pay for the wedding yourselves, neither family will shy away from expressing their opinion as to who should be footing the bill. Not surprisingly, this can lead to some disagreement.

Item That Needs to Be Paid for	What Groom's Family Says	What Bride's Family Says
Wedding dress	"Bride's family pays for it."	"That makes sense. We'll pay for the dress. No problem."
Flowers	"Bride's family pays for it."	"This seems like one of those expenses we could possibly split, but we'll be glad to pick up the tab here as well."
Rehearsal dinner	"Bride's family pays for it."	"Hmmmm. We thought the tradition was that the groom's family pays for this. What's going on here?"
Wedding reception	"Bride's family pays for it."	"Like we're really surprised. Thanks for the continued generosity, Ebenezer."
Groom's parents' hotel bill	"Bride's family pays for it."	"You guys can go to hell. Seriously."
New house for groom's family	"Bride's family pays for it."	"Honey, call the lawyer."

The good news is that your parents are now fighting with one another, rather than with you. So while the Montagues and the Capulets hash it out, you and your bride can slip away to Friar Laurence's den and tie the knot in secret. What could go wrong with that plan?

Knock Her Socks Off

When tensions between your fiancée and her mom boil over, the best thing you can do is just give your bride a hug and joke about how none of this would have happened if you hadn't bought her that silly diamond engagement ring. It's simple but very effective. When you were freaking out about the guest list (remember that?), your bride was there to comfort you. Now you have a chance to return the favor.

When tensions boil over between you and your parents, just do what every guy does: Completely ignore the problem and assume it will magically fix itself.

For the Bride

Ladies, while your fiancé will (hopefully) be more than willing to comfort you in your moments of stress, there's really no point in trying to explain or justify all of the mother-daughter issues to your man. It isn't that we're insensitive or don't care; we just have no possible basis for understanding what you're talking about.

When mothers try to become emotionally involved in their sons' lives, the dudes are usually oblivious. Rather than have a phone conversation with their mom about how they feel, guys will just play Xbox for thirty-six consecutive hours. As a result, our mothers simply shift their entire focus to our sisters. So, in a way, all this tension between you and your mother is our fault. We'd say we're sorry, but we're busy playing Grand Theft Auto. And you're blocking the TV—can you move?

10

Why Don't We Just Use E-vite?
Creating Your Wedding Invitations

Of all the events in the wedding-planning process, this is really the one where the groom is of absolutely no help. The world of fonts, embossed lettering, and lined envelopes is more complicated than a nuclear submarine.

Quick! Which of the following is a color that paper stock comes in?

1. Sunrise

2. Sheep's Milk

3. Jimmy Carter

4. Purple

It's a trick question. *They are all colors that paper stock comes in.* Now you understand what you're dealing with. Even if you have dabbled in creating your own letterhead, I still advise you to proceed with extreme caution. Drawing stick figures during a game of Pictionary doesn't suddenly make you Picasso.

The wedding invitation is, of course, a most important item. Without an invitation, no one would know when and where the wedding is taking place. Which means most of your guests wouldn't show up. Which means you'd save thousands of dollars on catering fees. So remind me again why we're having an invitation?

Here's a step-by-step breakdown of how the invitation process works (and by *breakdown* I'm referring to both the details of the design and the subsequent emotional state you'll be in):

STEP 1: SELECT YOUR PAPER

Sounds simple enough, which is why you should be nervous. There are many variables you'll have to take into account in selecting your paper, including:

- Paper color

- Paper size

- Paper thickness

- Paper price

- Are there matching envelopes?

- This is getting really complicated.

- Is the paper readily available?

- Is there a watermark on the paper?

- I need Advil.

- Does the paper take the ink well?

- Is the paper in stock?

- Vision blurry … can't breathe … call paramedics …

As you can see, selecting the paper is only slightly less complicated than the Apollo missions to the moon. And this is just step one.

STEP 2: ARGUE ABOUT THE TEXT OF THE INVITATION

This argument will be over whose names should be on the invitation. (Don't take for granted that your name will be one of them … everything is up for debate.) Traditionally, the parents of the bride have their names on the invites. Sometimes the parents of the groom like to have their names on the invitation as well. The bride's parents then counter by adding more names, and after several rounds of back-and-forth negotiations, you end up with an invitation that reads something like this:

Mr. And Mrs. Philip Anderson
and their good friend
Dr. James Morgan
and his patient
Ms. Angela Pierce
and her cat
Mr. Snuggles

Request the pleasure of your company
at the marriage of their daughter
Lisa Gail

to
Mr. Thomas Zimmerman

son of
Mr. Richard Zimmerman
Mrs. Lois Jordan

and her current husband
Mr. Steven Jordan

who is not related to former NBA star
Mr. Michael Jordan

whose longtime teammate was
Mr. Scottie Pippen

As for the text that tells people where and when the wedding is taking place, rest assured that there will also be squabbles about this part of the invitation. You and your bride will want the information to be as straightforward as possible. Your parents, however, want to be sure that the stupidest person on Earth can understand the invitation, so they insist that it reads as follows:

Saturday
the twenty-eighth of May
(It's Memorial Day weekend, although not Memorial
Day itself, which is a Monday)

at six o'clock
(p.m.)

The Meadow View Country Club
(*Not* the Meadow Valley Country Club—that one closed
down a year and a half ago.)

200 Jefferson Street
(If you're heading west on Main Street, you pass through
the center of town.
After Edna's House of Pies, there's an old red barn. Don't
turn yet. Go three more blocks
and look for the big sign that says
Meadow View Country Club.)

Phoenix,
Arizona
(It'll be like a thousand degrees.)

Dinner and dancing to follow

STEP 3: FIND OTHER DETAILS THAT YOU CAN LOSE SLEEP OVER

I doubt you'll need any help, but just in case:

- Should we get a calligrapher to address the envelopes?

- What color ink should the text be printed in?

- Should we specify a dress code on the invitation?

- Should we spell the bride's name correctly?

STEP 4: HAVE A TRAUMATIC EXPERIENCE WHEN YOU GO TO MAIL THE INVITATIONS

Mailing a bunch of envelopes seems so simple, which makes it all the more surprising when things go disastrously wrong. Before you showed up at the post office with all your invitations, you were smart enough to take in a sample envelope and have it weighed so you'd know what the postage would be. When you did this, though, you had not yet inserted a Xeroxed piece of paper with driving directions. Although this piece of paper weighs about a billionth of a pound, it's still enough to increase the postal rate. You remain blissfully unaware of this fact... until all the invitations are returned to you about two weeks later due to insufficient postage.

The Reply Card

When you mail the invitation (or rather, when you attempt to mail the invitation), it should include a reply card for your guests to return telling you whether or not they're coming.

Creating the reply card is much simpler than creating the invitation (because everything is much simpler than creating your invitation). The problem lies in what your guests will do with the reply card. The first thing they'll do is ignore whatever date you ask to have the cards returned by and assume you mean two to three weeks after that date. When you call to ask certain guests why they haven't returned their reply card yet, you usually get one of the following responses:

THE ALOOF RESPONSE

"I didn't even see that there was an RSVP date!"

THE MORONIC RESPONSE

"So how does this work, exactly? I send this bad boy back to you in the mail?"

THE ANGRY RESPONSE

"It's only a couple of days after the deadline. I don't see what the big deal is."

THE CONFUSING RESPONSE

"I didn't mail the card back to you. I mailed it to the caterer."

THE NONRESPONSE RESPONSE

"There's a 50 percent chance that I'm coming. Should I write that on the card?"

THE TRYING-TO-DISTRACT-YOU-WITH-A-COMPLIMENT RESPONSE

"I guess I was just so distracted by the beauty of the invitation that I forgot to RSVP." (Note: The Trying-to-Distract-You-with-a-Compliment response works very well.)

THE HONEST RESPONSE
"I lost it."

None of the responses actually involves telling you definitively whether or not the person is attending your wedding. This is because of the following really annoying fact:

Really Annoying Fact

Most people don't truly decide if they are coming to your wedding until the night before the event.

In a way, the people who don't RSVP are doing you a favor. They're undecided because they need to wait and see what else is going on that weekend: They may have family in from out of town; they may have a business trip; they may want to stay home and watch the Food Network.

The real shock is that the people who actually did send in their reply cards are also undecided. They've checked off a box and mailed back the card so that you don't yell at them, but this represents no actual commitment in their minds. They'll give you their final decision via phone two to three days before the wedding, which is well after you've given the final head count to the caterer.

Getting this final number for the caterer, incidentally, is no easy task. As noted, many cards won't be returned, and at least half of those that are will have an unhelpful message like, "We'll be there!!!!!!!" There will be no indication as to the iden-

tity of the sender, so you spend days analyzing the handwriting
and looking at the postmark until you finally determine that
your co-worker Dan (and his date) can make it to your wedding. That is, until he cancels.

Tip of the Iceberg

You are allowed, under state law, to have up to 1.6 trillion stationery items per wedding, so the invitation is merely the beginning.

SAVE-THE-DATE CARDS

You send out save-the-date cards a few months before the
invitation so that people can make room in their long-term
plans for your wedding. And since your friends can't plan
anything beyond next Wednesday, they simply throw away
the save-the-date card.

THANK-YOU NOTES

Your bride will probably want to order thank-you notes
with both of your names printed on them. This sounds fine to
you, until you realize that there's a good chance these notes
will be pink, and you'll have to send one to your brother.

REHEARSAL DINNER INVITATIONS

These don't need to be as fancy as your wedding invitation. Then again, Congressional Medals of Honor aren't as
fancy as your wedding invitation.

PROGRAMS

It's nice to print up a program for the wedding ceremony so the guests have something to read instead of having to pay attention to your vows.

DINNER MENUS

Your guests will want to know what they'll be having for dinner at the reception, so they can be sure and tell you that they would have picked something different.

PLACE CARDS

Place cards are helpful because come dinnertime, you'll know exactly where everyone will be. It's sort of like giving all your guests one of those electronic ankle bracelets they make people wear when they're under house arrest. So when Aunt Linda asks if you've seen Uncle Bob, you can look at your computer and tell her he's over at Table 9 for the moment, but he'll need to be back in his cell in time for lockdown.

Side Effects

Even the gruffest guy will develop an appreciation for fine stationery by the end of his wedding. This is not an entirely good thing, though. Certainly, your wife will be thrilled. However, there will be awkward moments with some of your single guy friends, who have not yet learned the beauty of off-set printing.

For example, you'll be visiting one of these dudes a few days after you've mailed out your wedding invitations (or remailed them, as the case may be). You notice that the dude has thrown away the envelope that the invitation came in. A few months ago, throwing away the envelope would have seemed perfectly logical to you as well. The envelope has performed its job admirably and can now be laid to rest.

That was the old you, though. The new you is aware of how much time, energy, and money went into creating that envelope:

- three dollars for the envelope itself

- two dollars to get your return address printed on the back of the envelope

- three dollars to get a calligrapher to write the destination address on the front of the envelope

- one dollar in postage

That's a nine-dollar envelope (not even counting the failed mailings). Nine dollars! That's two pints of beer! In your mind, this friend should appreciate the envelope for at least three months before throwing it away. So while he's in the bathroom, you take the envelope out of the trash, wipe away the spaghetti sauce stain, and put the envelope on his fridge.

Knock Her Socks Off

All joking aside, you and your bride really will get a few anonymous RSVP cards in the mail. So what do you do? The trick is to write a number, in pencil, on the back of each card before you send it out. Pair each number with a guest's name. Then if you get an anonymous card, flip it over, look at the number, and refer to your list of names and numbers to figure out who sent it. It's a lot more accurate than guessing. And it's a lot cheaper than opening up a *CSI: Weddings* lab and dusting the cards for fingerprints.

If you're worried that your local post office may be unreliable, you can mail an invitation to yourself. If it arrives at your home a day later in one piece, you'll know that all the invites went out okay. If the invitation arrives in pieces three weeks later, you'll know it's time to activate the emergency phone tree.

For the Bride

It's important to get your fiancé involved in stationery decisions. Unlike the issues with your mother, this is a topic that guys don't know a lot about but could learn to love. A married gentleman should know a thing or two about stationery, since we're past the age when we can send thank-you notes written on napkins.

Just because we *should* know something, though, doesn't mean we'll embrace it with open arms. So treat us like a five-year-old if you must: Drag us along, show us the pretty colors, watch us smile, and then buy us an ice-cream cone. What a special day!

11

Why Is Everyone Suddenly Acting Like a Moron?
Dealing with Out-of-Town Guests

There is some magical spell that weddings cast on people—perhaps the joy of the occasion—that makes them somehow unable to plan their weekend trip to your nuptials without extreme difficulty. And I'm not talking about your elderly grandparents who haven't been on a plane in years. They've actually been saving up their frequent-flier miles and know just what to do. Rather, it's the young professionals in their thirties and forties, who travel six days a week for business, who will be absolutely mystified as to how to get to your wedding, even if it's being held at the Airport Hilton in Chicago.

What's more, you've actually provided travel information that a baby giraffe could understand. Yet you can still expect the following conversation:

FRIEND: I got that thing you sent me about where to stay. Should I stay at that hotel?

YOU: Yes.

FRIEND: Should I stay somewhere else?

YOU: No.

FRIEND: So the wedding is in Miami, right?

YOU: Yes.

FRIEND: What airport should I use?

YOU: The one in Miami.

FRIEND: I found a great airfare on the Internet, but I'll have to fly into Orlando.

YOU: Orlando is in another part of the state, several hours away.

FRIEND: So, should I buy the ticket?

YOU: You can if you want, but then you'll have to get from Orlando to Miami.

FRIEND: How?

YOU: Rent a car, maybe.

FRIEND: How do I do that?

The Hotel Block

Even though some out-of-town guests seem to expect far too much from you when it comes to arranging travel plans and accommodations, there are nonetheless several responsibilities you and your bride must assume on their behalf. First and foremost is blocking off hotel rooms.

If you're having a rural wedding, the traditional thing to do is select a charming country inn that has about twelve rooms, and then let your 150 out-of-town guests fight over them.

If you're having an urban wedding, the traditional thing to do is select two hotels: the most expensive one in town and the crappiest one in town. Do not, under any circumstances, pick a moderately priced hotel that everyone can stay at, even though this makes perfect sense.

No matter which hotels you use, you'll quickly discover that they are not particularly good at being hotels. If you're not quite sure what I mean, here's a list of the things you'd think a hotel would be able to do.

Things a Hotel Would Probably Be Able to Do, Because, After All, It's a Hotel

1. Take room reservations

2. Remember room reservations once they've taken them

3. Modify and cancel room reservations

4. Remember how much the rooms cost

5. Remember how many rooms they have in the hotel

6. Not be totally confused by people who have the same last name but different first names

7. Not be totally confused by everything in the entire world

Right off the bat, the hotel will deny that you have ever set up a room block, even if you did it five minutes ago. It's as though you're in an episode of *The Twilight Zone*.

Next, the hotel moves on to phase two: ignoring the price they quoted you. Though you put the rate the hotel gave you on your save-the-date cards ($149 a night), when your friends call the hotel, the hotel tells them it's $279 a night. You call to investigate, and the hotel tries to convince you that $279 is a great rate. You tell the hotel that you were quoted $149. The hotel tells you that to get $149 a night, you'll need to reserve a block of rooms. And then your head explodes.

Once the hotel finds the room block (again), they'll take the number of rooms you've reserved and remove 50 percent of them. Maybe this is some sort of bizarre tax—the government needs 50 percent of all room blocks to go to them. Regardless, the block will be full after the fifth person calls, even though you've reserved eighty-five rooms.

Those friends of yours lucky enough to get a reservation will then be in the unenviable position of having to deal with the hotel themselves. You already know about the hotel's bizarre customer service, but it comes as a shock to your friends when they ask the woman at the front desk if she can tell them the checkout time and she responds by saying no.

The Welcome Basket

The guests who actually make it to the hotel with their room intact deserve some sort of a reward. While not a necessity, a welcome basket from you in their hotel room is a nice gesture. Here's what's typically in such a basket.

A WELCOME LETTER FROM THE BRIDE AND GROOM

It should go something like this:

Hi! And welcome to our wedding weekend! Every sentence in this letter is going to end with an exclamation point!

We hope the information in this packet is helpful! If it isn't, we're sure Uncle Bob will tell us so in no uncertain terms!

If there's anything we can do to make the weekend more enjoyable, just let us know! And by "us" we mean "anyone besides us," because we're getting married tomorrow and are on the verge of a total meltdown!!

Fondly,

Bride and Groom!

FOOD AND DRINK

You don't need anything fancy—just some snacks and maybe a bottle of water. Yes, the hotel said each room has a minibar, but are you really going to believe the hotel at this point? They also claimed all the rooms had amenities like hot water and windows.

SCHEDULE OF EVENTS

You don't want too much detail here, since it will probably confuse people. Just spell out the highlights:

Thursday evening,	
5:00 P.M.:	You arrive at the wedding weekend a day early, expecting there to be an activity tonight, even though we told you there wouldn't be.
Friday evening,	
4:45 P.M.:	Despite the fact that the rehearsal dinner starts at 6:00 p.m., this is the time you'll actually show up so that you can take full advantage of the free shrimp cocktail and open bar.
Saturday,	
9:00 A.M. to 4:00 P.M.:	As the bride and groom frantically get ready for the wedding ceremony, this is the traditional time when you should call us with trivial matters like, "I forgot my Advil" or "Which way is east?"

Saturday evening,

5:00 P.M.:	Ceremony starts.
5:20 P.M.:	Majority of guests arrive, because "this place is so hard to find" even though they are staying in the hotel where the wedding is taking place.

Sunday,

11:45 A.M.:	Departure time for your flight home.
2:18 P.M.:	This is when you show up at the bride and groom's house and tell them that you missed your flight home and ask if you can crash with them.

Monday,

noon:	Seriously. You have to go home now.

A MAP OF THE AREA AND INFORMATION ON LOCAL SIGHTS

You should point out the city's most famous attractions (museums, historical landmarks, Starbucks) as well as some places off the beaten path. For example:

If you take a left out of the hotel, you'll soon be on Lincoln Ave. This is the oldest street in the city and was originally a residential area for the upper classes. Now it's overrun with hookers and junkies. We recommend Silvia for the sex and Eddie if you're looking to score drugs!

One More Meal

The final thing you can do for your out-of-town guests is schedule a brunch for the morning after the wedding. This is a relatively new tradition that came about via powerful wedding-guest lobbyists in Washington, D.C., who saw an opportunity to squeeze one more meal out of the bride and groom before returning home.

If you're on the fence about spending the money on a brunch, consider the following pros and cons.

Reason to Have the Brunch	Reason Not to Have the Brunch
Chance to say goodbye to your nephew who lives in North Dakota.	After he stole the microphone from the bandleader so he could amplify his burps, do you really want to say anything to him?
Bride and groom were so busy during the wedding reception, they didn't get a chance to eat dinner and are now really hungry.	Appetite ruined when everyone starts asking when you're having kids.
You can talk to some of the guests you didn't really have a chance to see the night before.	Those guests confess that they didn't actually make it to the wedding because they discovered they could order porn in their hotel room.
Guests will appreciate the hospitality.	Guests will abuse hospitality and ask, "So, when's lunch?"

Reason to Have the Brunch	Reason Not to Have the Brunch
After a night of partying, you could use a strong cup of coffee.	After a night of partying, you're still quite drunk, and a cup of coffee ain't hiding it.
Omelet station!	It costs thirty-one dollars per omelet!

A Rival Affair

Having made all these detailed arrangements for your out-of-town guests, you and your bride will be crestfallen to learn that some of these people won't be able to attend the wedding. There's the range of normal reasons—can't get the time off from work, too expensive, don't really like you—but you soon learn that there is also a rival wedding on the same weekend as your event.

The rival wedding belongs to someone you know but aren't really friends with. While you had no expectation of being invited to the rival groom's wedding, there are going to be a dozen overlaps on the two guest lists. You figure it won't be that big a deal. Half the overlaps will come to your wedding and half will go to his.

Then, the first four overlaps all decide to go to the other dude's wedding and you immediately freak out. Even though you have more people coming to your event than you know what to do with, you begin a vigorous campaign to get the eight remaining overlaps to come to your wedding. You tell them that they will have the finest table assignments; you announce you'll be serving their favorite entrée at dinner; you offer a "backstage pass" so they can hang out and get high with the wedding band at the end of the night.

When none of this works, you draw a line in the sand and put your friends in a really awkward position. You make it clear that in choosing which wedding they attend, they'll also be choosing which groom they want to be friends with. Since you are acting irrational and crazy, it's an easy decision for them. Off they go to the rival groom's wedding.

The upside is that your hotel had already canceled the room reservations for these overlap guests, even though no one told the hotel to do this.

Knock Her Socks Off

Besides cost and location, one of the main factors you should consider when choosing a hotel for your out-of-town guests is their particular policy for blocking off rooms. Not all hotels do this the same way. Some will insist that the bride and groom pay for any rooms in the block that aren't reserved. Other hotels will just release the extra rooms from the block at a specified date and then rent out those unused rooms to the general public. The second policy is obviously preferable, since it's impossible to predict exactly how many rooms you'll need.

It's also a good idea to call the hotel periodically and see how many rooms are left in your block. You may want to add more rooms if the block is getting full. The hotel may do this automatically, but it's a good idea to double-check.

For the Bride

Oftentimes, your groom will get overly frustrated from his dealings with the out-of-town guests. If that's the case, you should remind him that in the future you two will be the ones traveling to weddings and you'll both inexplicably turn into morons at that time. So be nice, or you won't get any sympathy down the road when you call up your friend and say, "We're coming to your wedding in Paris. Is there anything to see in that city?"

12

Um . . . Sweetie, Are You Okay?

*An Interlude While Your Bride (and You)
Have a Quick Meltdown*

You're more than halfway home with the planning at this point and you and your bride are both feeling pretty good about everything. Yes, you've reserved a venue you don't really like, fought multiple times with your parents, and are about 7,000 percent over budget. Nonetheless, you have survived these bumps in the road and you're still standing. You've even managed to convince yourself that the tasks you haven't yet completed—picking out the food, planning the honeymoon—are the fun part of wedding planning and something to look forward to. And when you say "fun part of the wedding planning" you mean "just as complicated as everything else except maybe it won't involve my parents telling me we have to invite the crazy lady who watches their Irish setter when they go skiing."

Given that things are generally going well, there's no

reason to think either of you will have a breakdown. Which naturally means you're both on the precipice of a really big one.

Weddings vs. Thunderstorms

To better understand this peculiar moment in the planning process, it helps to compare weddings to thunderstorms. I grew up in New England, and every evening during the humid summer months there would be a brief thunderstorm. They're loud. They're scary. But once they pass, something magic happens. Even though everyone knows that more bad weather is on the way tomorrow, the collective mood still brightens. You open your windows; you move your patio furniture back outside; you listen to your dad declare that the pool water is totally safe for swimming even though he has no idea what he's talking about.

The wedding planning has similar moments when the storm has passed and all is looking bright. Rather than celebrate, however, your bride is concerned. She has probably lived through a thunderstorm and so knows what to expect when they roll into town. The wedding, by contrast, is still uncharted territory, and that makes her nervous. As a result, the two of you will likely have the following conversation one night as you both lie in bed reading:

GROOM: I'm really enjoying this Shaquille O'Neal biography!

BRIDE: We don't have enough.

GROOM: What are you talking about? Enough what?

BRIDE: Chairs. For the reception. We're not going to have enough chairs.

GROOM: We haven't even discussed chairs yet. How do you know we won't have enough?

BRIDE: I can't believe it! We messed up with the chairs! It's so simple! So obvious! Chairs!

GROOM: We still have three months until the wedding. I'm sure there's plenty of time to solve the chair problem. You know Shaquille O'Neal always says...

[*Bride bursts into tears.*]

BRIDE: Says what?! What does Shaq say about wedding chairs that could possibly be helpful?! That we're totally screwed since we don't have enough? Because that's the reality! No matter how many championships Shaq has won!

GROOM: I think I'm ready for bed.

Your bride's reaction may seem crazy at the time (because, seriously, Shaq's championships are really quite impressive). In truth, however, your fiancée is just letting off a little wedding-planning steam. That's it. It's nothing to worry about. In fact, you should worry if your bride *doesn't* do this. It's better for her to have a minor freak-out about the chairs now than to explode in a few months. Such an explosion will result in her having a torrid affair with a handsome furniture manufacturer because "he knows what I need." Namely, chairs.

Moreover, the releasing of wedding-planning steam comes and goes quickly. The following morning, your bride will be back to normal.

By the way, for all the differences between weddings and thunderstorms, there are a few interesting similarities between the two phenomena:

Interesting Similarities Between Thunderstorms and Weddings

1. Labor Day weekend is a popular time for both events.

2. In the moments before each event arrives, people look around nervously and say, "It's getting closer!"

3. They can both wreak havoc on your ability to attend the Dodgers-Giants game this weekend.

4. During both events, you are ultimately at the mercy of either Mother Nature or the mother of the bride.

A Contagious Disease

Postmeltdown, your bride is doing much better. Suddenly, though, *you're* starting to feel a little anxious. Your bride has accidentally passed her meltdown on to you as though it were a head cold. You spend most of the next day thinking about the chairs.

Were you too hasty in assuming that there was an easy fix? If there's a shortage, how will you decide who stands during the ceremony? Is it possible to import chairs from some foreign country that is rich in this precious resource?

By the time you get into bed the following night, the transference is complete. While your bride tries to read her Toni Morrison book, you start screaming about the chairs. She wisely ignores your panic, gently tells you to relax, and turns out the light. The next morning you feel much better, just as your bride did the day before. You remove all the anxious thoughts from your mind and go about your business.

Of course, when the wedding finally does roll around, you're fifty chairs short.

Subsequent Five-Minute Meltdowns

Although the eye of the planning is the time when most couples share a quick and enjoyable meltdown, it's not necessarily the only moment when this will happen. If you and your bride felt greatly relieved after your first meltdown, then you may employ additional meltdowns throughout the remainder of your planning. Some folks relax with yoga; others get massages; a few may even employ some "retail therapy" to ease their tension. But *everyone* finds the time to unwind with a few five-minute meltdowns now and then.

Although the meltdowns are ultimately benign, it's still best to have them in the privacy of your own home if possible.

If your parents see you freaking out, they will assume that you are both having second thoughts about getting married. In truth, you and your bride's love for each other is the only thing that *isn't* causing you stress. Long-term happiness? Not a concern. The caterer hasn't returned your most recent phone call? It's time to camp outside the therapist's office until your next appointment.

Your parents, though, may refuse to accept the fact that you aren't having problems. They might try to help by suggesting other people that you could marry: "What about that cute blond girl you went to elementary school with?"

There can also be problems if other people besides your parents see you stressed out. If your planner sees you and your bride having a meltdown, she will think that she's not doing her job very well. This, in turn, will cause her to have a meltdown. The planner's parents will then assume that she is upset because her marriage is on the rocks. They'll chime in with other people they think the planner could marry.

If your friends or co-workers see you stressed out, they will offer unhelpful suggestions like, "Don't stress out." You will then turn into that Jack Nicholson character from *A Few Good Men* and shout something confrontational, such as: "You have the luxury of not knowing what I know about wedding photographers!"

In truth, only couples who have been married in the last five years can properly appreciate the five-minute meltdown. These couples are your allies. They know that a little freaking out about the guest list is a good and healthy occurrence. They will try to ease your mind by telling you that there's one thing they wish they could change about their own wedding: not to have worried about it as much as they did. Also, they wish they'd had more chairs.

Knock Her Socks Off

If you and your bride are going through a bit of a meltdown epidemic, one of the best things you can do is take a mini-vacation. Many people are reluctant to do this because they are going away right after the wedding and money is probably tight. The minivacation, though, doesn't have to be expensive. See if you can borrow your parents' lake house or your uncle's ski cabin for the night. Even if you don't ski (or hate lakes), the change of scenery will do wonders for your stress level.

For the Bride

Ladies, one of the biggest mistakes you can make in trying to combat meltdowns is institute a we're-not-going-to-talk-about-the-wedding-for-the-rest-of-the-day edict. Your fiancé is going to violate this edict almost immediately. He's not trying to spite you. Rather, he'll accidentally say something like, "Look, we got a reply card in the mail," and that will be all it takes. Then you'll both get stressed out about violating the edict, which causes a subsequent five-minute meltdown.

Thus, in trying to fix the problem, you've inadvertently made it worse. It's far better to issue edicts that you know you both can obey, even if they're sort of stupid. Instead of saying, "We're not talking about the wedding for the rest of the day," have an edict that says, "We're not talking about Russian history for the rest of the day." You'll both observe the edict, because neither one of you knows anything about Russian history and weren't going to be talking about it anyway. You'll go to bed happy and feel as though you are in control of your life, which, of course, you're not.

13

Should My Finger Be Turning Blue?
Selecting Your Wedding Rings

Most guys have never worn a ring in their life. Or, if they have, it was some sort of my-team-won-the-world-championship ring, worn primarily in the hopes of picking up undergraduate women. Your wedding ring, by contrast, signals an important shift toward maturity. You are now a sophisticated gentleman, proudly wearing an expensive ring on your finger. Of course, if someone dares you to shove the ring up your nostril for five bucks, you'll do it.

The Search Begins

Before you select *your* wedding ring, you'll first want to see what kind of ring your fiancée has in mind for herself. The length of time it takes to find her ring depends on who purchased the engagement ring.

If you bought your bride's engagement ring on your own, she'll probably want to spend a lot of time shopping for her wedding band, because she hasn't been ring shopping yet.

If she went shopping for her engagement ring with you, she'll now have a passion and a thirst for jewelry, so she'll still want to spend a lot of time shopping for the band. Thus, no matter how you got the engagement ring, you'll spend every Saturday until the wedding at the jewelry store.

It's important that you be with your bride during these lengthy shopping experiences, because the wedding rings are a representation of the love you feel for each other. Also, you have to pay for them.

Shopping for your bride's wedding ring occurs in three phases.

PHASE 1: TRY ON EVERY WEDDING RING CURRENTLY IN EXISTENCE

This phase is necessary in order to find the band that best complements the lovely engagement ring you gave your fiancée. Although, if that's true, why is she currently trying on earrings and bracelets?

PHASE 2: CONTEMPLATE GETTING A NEW WEDDING RING THAT'S MADE SPECIFICALLY TO GO WITH HER ENGAGEMENT RING

The problem with every existing ring is, quite simply, that it already exists. Getting a new, one-of-a-kind, custom-made wedding ring assures a uniqueness to her hardware that is both exciting and desirable. By the way, the jeweler may fail to mention that the ring comes from a mold that he uses to churn out twelve hundred "one-of-a-kind" rings every month.

PHASE 3: PURCHASE MULTIPLE WEDDING RINGS

The choice between a custom-made ring and an existing ring is too difficult. So why make it?

The Lord of His Ring

Now that your lady is taken care of, it's time to turn your attention toward finding a ring for yourself. The first decision to make is whether you want to get a ring that matches your bride's (or, at least, matches *one* of her rings). This depends largely on what sort of ring your bride decided on. If she got a simple gold or platinum band, you're in business. If she got a diamond-and-sapphire-studded baby that could light up Times Square, you should probably hesitate before getting that sort of man-bling for yourself.

Whatever type of ring you decide you're in the market for, the shopping process will again occur in three phases. Not surprisingly, though, these phases differ dramatically from the ones your bride went through.

PHASE 1: SPEND LESS THAN TWO MINUTES TRYING ON RINGS BEFORE REACHING A DECISION

"Let me see that simple platinum one. Yep, looks great. I'll take it."

PHASE 2: FREAK OUT THAT YOU CAN'T GET THE RING OFF YOUR FINGER

The jeweler will have sized your ring perfectly, which means it is snug so it doesn't fall off your finger when you're taking a shower or eating soup. It also means that it takes more than two seconds to remove the ring from your finger, which will give you a heart attack. Moreover, since you've had the ring in your possession for under a minute, no one has shown you the proper way to remove a ring. Pulling as hard as you can is the *incorrect* way. You need to bend your finger slightly and ease the ring back and forth over the knuckle. Of course, it's too late for that now. Your finger is blue and swollen. Convinced that the ring will never come off, you demand bolt cutters, an ambulance, and your lawyer.

PHASE 3: RESIZE THE RING A MINIMUM OF FIFTY-THREE TIMES BEFORE THE WEDDING DAY

The jeweler informs you he can resize the ring, so you cancel the bolt cutters and the ambulance.

He enlarges the ring, making it big enough to be worn as a bracelet. You are thrilled. You take the ring home, try it on, and notice that even Krazy Glue won't keep the ring on your finger. Thus begin months of back-and-forth trips to the jeweler to get the ring resized. Eventually, the metal in the ring gets overworked and cracks in half. You have to get a brand-new ring and repeat all three phases.

Dress Rehearsal

Even if the ring fits perfectly, it's still a good idea to wear it around the house a few times before the wedding, because it can take some getting used to. Inevitably, your mother will stop by while you are wearing the ring. She'll notice the ring and then have a total meltdown: "You ran off and got married without telling me! How could you do that?" Eventually, you calm her down and tell her that you just picked up the ring from the jeweler and were merely trying it on. This, in turn, triggers another meltdown from your mother: "You went and picked out your ring without telling me! How could you do that?"

There are a few key lessons about the ring that you'll learn when you wear it around the house during this dress rehearsal period.

Key Lesson About the Ring	How You Will Learn This Lesson
Unlike the rings you had when you were eight years old, this ring is not made of candy.	The hard way.
It is heavier than you think.	You keep swerving into walls until your inner ear begins to compensate.
Spinning it on a tabletop is incredibly cool.	Your married buddy shows you this trick one night when your wives are out watching a movie that stars Hugh Grant and/or Colin Firth.

Key Lesson About the Ring	How You Will Learn This Lesson
You won't be able to stop fidgeting with it.	You spend so much time rubbing the ring and smiling wickedly that you begin to resemble a Bond villain.
You can hurt somebody with it.	When you lean over to kiss your fiancée good night, the ring slides off your finger and lands in her eye.
The minute you take it off, you'll lose it.	You're repeatedly looking under the couch and saying, "Dammit! I just had it a second ago!"

Words for All Eternity

Before you hand your rings over to your best man so that he can misplace them, there's one final decision you and your bride must make: to engrave or not to engrave. Engraving is relatively inexpensive and makes the rings more special. The hard part is deciding what words you are going to engrave. You'll have to read these words for all eternity. So while you both love the lyrics to the Rolling Stones' "Sympathy for the Devil," they may lack that forever-yours quality you're after.

Even if there is a poem or phrase that you both think is appropriate, it may not fit on the ring. Or rather, it may not fit on her ring, since your ring has been slowly resized to have the diameter of a Michelin tire. You may have to shorten the phrase, which could alter its meaning. Let's say the engraving on your bride's ring is supposed to read: "Darling, I'll love you more than any man ever will." But the phrase gets a whole new meaning when it's shortened, suddenly making it sound as though you might be bisexual: "Darling, I'll love you more than any man."

The solution for most couples is to just engrave their initials and the wedding date. You can run into trouble here as well, however, especially if the woman is changing her name. Let's say the bride's maiden name is Parker Ursula King and she's marrying Oliver Nelson McKenzie Everett. Her new name will be Parker Ursula King-Everett.

When you go to get the rings engraved, Parker writes down her new initials and suddenly realizes that they spell PUKE. Worse, when combined with Oliver's initials, they spell PUKE ON ME. Oliver suggests Parker drop the Ursula from her name, but every woman in her family has been named Ursula, dating back to the Civil War. Additionally, Parker's dad would be crestfallen if she dropped the Everett. So Parker and Oliver wind up engraving the lyrics to "Sympathy for the Devil" on the inside of their rings as a compromise. And for all of eternity, Parker's ring reads, PLEASED TO MEET YOU, HOPE YOU GUESS MY NAME, which sort of makes her sound like a hooker. But at least that's better than PUKE ON ME.

Safekeeping

Now that you have the rings, you'll need to find a safe place to keep them until the wedding ceremony. Consider the following options.

SOMEWHERE SAFE IN THE HOUSE

Since most people don't have a proper safe in the house, "someplace safe" usually means the dresser drawer where you put important stuff like jewelry, Altoids, and a piece of paper that has a hundred random phone numbers scribbled on it.

The rings are going to be fairly safe in the drawer. The problem is that your bride will want to continually try her ring on, and at some point she'll forget to put it back in the safe drawer. Which means on the day of the wedding, you have to rummage through all the other drawers in your house, including the drawer with the take-out menus, the drawer where the Scotch tape and scissors are supposed to be (but they're not), and the drawer that never opens, so you have to pull on it for twenty minutes, at which time it breaks.

GIVE THEM TO YOUR BEST MAN

You're not entirely sure that your best man can be trusted with the rings during the ceremony, so this is a precarious option. It's worth considering, however, because if he loses them, at least it's not your fault.

SAFE-DEPOSIT BOX

If only you could find the key to your safe-deposit box. It's supposed to be in the drawer with the Scotch tape ...

AT YOUR PARENTS' HOUSE

Not as smart as it sounds. The rings will be used as ransom in order to squeeze four more random people onto the guest list: "You want the ring?! Guy Flenderson and his girlfriend better be at Table 9!"

Finally, you come up with the best idea yet: You'll simply pick the rings up from the jeweler a few days before the wedding. Genius! Unfortunately, you show up at the store and realize the jeweler is in South Africa for the next six weeks.

Knock Her Socks Off

All joking aside, if your bride is indeed intrigued by several different wedding rings, take note. While only one ring will be the official one, lots of women accumulate additional rings over the years to wear on other fingers or to stack next to the engagement ring. Therefore, you have a gift list that you can use on anniversaries, important birthdays, etc. There's no safer present in the world than a piece of jewelry that your wife has already told you she likes.

For the Bride

A lot of women get freaked out when their fiancés ask to have their weddings rings enlarged so they can be removed easily. Brides tend to say things like, "It's not supposed to come off easily!" as though the groom is somehow planning to have a lot of extramarital affairs and wants to be sure the wedding ring won't cramp his style.

Relax. For one of the few moments in our life, we're really *not* thinking about sex. We're simply thinking about the hospital having to chop off our finger in order to remove the ring.

Just give us a few days to adjust to our new piece of jewelry. We love you, and we'd never dream of cheating. And, yes, we're well aware that if we did, our finger wouldn't be the only thing getting chopped off.

14

The Airlines Charge People for Meals Now, so Why Can't We?
Selecting the Dinner Menu

No matter how much food you order, it will not be enough. Your guests have spent several hundred dollars on gifts and travel, and they view dinner as the moment for them to recoup their losses.

In particular, hors d'oeuvres will be consumed as if America's freedom is at stake. This is because your guests have just sat through your wedding ceremony, which has inevitably run long, probably because one of the people you asked to read a poem went off on an improvised tangent about themselves. By the end, your guests are so hungry that they will knock over the bride to get to the food.

If you're having one hundred wedding guests, here's the quantity of hors d'oeuvres that your caterer will recommend vs. the amount you will actually need.

Item	Quantity Caterer Recommends	Quantity You Will Actually Need
Pigs in a blanket	100	5,791
Crab cakes	One per person	Twenty-three per person
Chicken on skewers	200 skewers	At least 50 extra, because the male guests will need supplies for their skewer-fight tournament
Shrimp cocktail	10 pounds	Drain the Pacific Ocean, baby!
Crudités	A whole station featuring 15 to 20 different platters of seasonal fresh produce	0

Every time a waiter comes out of the kitchen with a plate of hors d'oeuvres, people swarm around him, eat every ounce of food on his tray in under three seconds, and then leave him for dead. The waiter returns to the kitchen a battered man. The maitre d' quickly patches him up, like a boxing trainer in between rounds. Then a bell sounds, the waiter inserts his mouth guard, and the maitre d' sends him back into the ring.

The Tasting

Once the hors d'oeuvre quantities have been successfully misordered, you'll have a chance to taste all the different entrées that your caterer has to offer. The food at the tasting will:

1. be delicious.

2. in no way resemble the food that will be served at the wedding, because the caterer knows you will be too busy on your wedding day to eat any of the food, so he can bring in whatever he wants.

Nevertheless, a decision on the entrée has to be made. Most people assume they must pick one of the "big three" wedding entrées: chicken, steak, or fish. This is shortsighted, however, because your caterer will also offer you some creative alternatives.

Creative Alternative Offered by the Caterer	Pro	Con
Venison	Hearty and flavorful.	At least one person will stand up and shout, "You killed Bambi!"
Lobster	A delicacy.	Claw fights!

Creative Alternative Offered by the Caterer	Pro	Con
Veggie burgers	Superhealthy.	Everyone will hate you. Seriously.
Middle Eastern food	Exotic and yummy.	Launches an angry debate about U.S. foreign policy.
Duck	Sophisticated and elegant.	Annoying friend of your parents spends the rest of the night making quacking noises in an attempt to be funny.
Sweetbreads	They sound delicious!	Do you know what these are?
Bean-and-cheese burritos	No one goes home hungry.	No one goes home at all. People just sort of sit on the floor, rubbing their stomachs and moaning in pain.

Okay, so the decision really is between chicken, steak, and fish. The caterer will do all three of these entrées well. If you can't decide what to serve, you can offer your guests a choice. However, this usually requires that your guests specify on their reply card which entrée they'll want for dinner. Even if you've clearly indicated that the choice is between filet of beef and salmon, your guests will take this opportunity to tell you their fantasy meal, requesting items such as frogs' legs, slow-roasted loin of veal, and caviar.

It's nice to have a vegetarian option for your guests as well. You can't accommodate everyone's dietary quirks ("I don't eat food that's orange!"), but a vegetarian option covers the needs of most people. Luckily, the caterer says he offers a delicious vegetarian option. However, the day of the wedding you notice that the vegetarian option is simply the side starch and vegetable minus the entrée. And since there are bacon bits on the baked potato and the vegetables were simmered in chicken stock, your vegetarian friends can't eat it anyway.

The Rest of the Meal

With the entrée in place, it's time to decide what else your guests will be dining on. If the caterer is smart, he's gotten everyone at the tasting drunk by now, so these other food decisions tend to be quick and jovial.

THE APPETIZER

It doesn't take long for you to figure out that the first-course options are just supersized hors d'oeuvres. Instead of tiny crab cakes, you can serve a large crab cake; instead of individual pieces of fried shrimp, you can serve five pieces of fried shrimp; instead of one massive raw vegetable plate that no one will touch, you can have two hundred small raw vegetable plates that no one will touch. The good news is that most of your guests will not have tried the hors d'oeuvres because, as you recall, you didn't order enough of them. Any appetizer course will be welcomed with open arms.

THE SALAD

The caterer will offer you three or four different salads to choose from, all of which are exactly the same, except for the dressing.

THE BREAD

The bread tastes...like bread.

DESSERT

Since the caterer isn't making the cake, he will encourage you to serve a separate dessert in addition to the cake. This is just an attempt to get you to spend more money. It works perfectly. There is no such thing as too much dessert.

The Big Decision

Now that the menu is set, you'll need to decide whether to have a buffet or table service. Here's how the night will play out, depending on which style you choose.

BEFORE DINNER (DURING THE WEDDING CEREMONY)

Buffet	Table Service
The caterer decides to set up the buffet carving station as you are exchanging vows, meaning everyone in attendance stares at	The caterer needs to move tables to make space for the waiters to walk around them; this results in a massive collision between

Buffet	Table Service
the ten-pound prime rib instead of watching the ceremony.	two tables, which releases a sound resembling the Hindenburg explosion. This crash happens at the precise moment your friend is singing "Amazing Grace."

DURING DINNER

Buffet	Table Service
Within four seconds of the waiters taking the lids off the buffet trays, a line begins forming that quickly rivals the one at Space Mountain during school vacation.	Despite the fact that the caterer insisted you tell him precisely how many people were having steak and how many were having fish, he immediately runs out of steak and begins serving everyone the vegetarian entrée.

AFTER DINNER

Buffet	Table Service
The fire department is called when the caterer attempts to extinguish buffet table Sternos with water and accidentally spreads a napalmlike substance all over the bride's dress.	You notice that all the waiters are eating steak for dinner. When you ask the caterer about this, he says, defensively: "We were going to eat the vegetarian entrée, but we had to serve that to all your guests."

The Only Part of the Wedding
That Really Matters

With the food decision in the books, it's time to turn your attention to the moment you've been waiting for since you got engaged: the booze. Most grooms desperately want to seize control of this part of the wedding planning, because they have "the craziest friends ever" and they're "totally gonna get plastered." No one has yet told the groom that:

1. This is not something to brag about.

2. It's going to cost a ton of money.

3. Those "crazy" friends aren't going to be invited anyway.

However, since you, the groom, are now speaking with a passion that resembles Sir Laurence Olivier delivering a Shakespearean monologue, everyone lets you have your moment in the sun.

Many people choose to have an open bar, which means your grateful guests will come up to you throughout the night with drunken praise such as: "This wedding is *awesome!*" and "Seriously, dude, this wedding is *awesome!*" However, it can be difficult to estimate the cost of having an open bar. Essentially, the caterer keeps a running tab of what everyone drinks throughout the night. Then, at the end of the party, he simply adds up the tab and hands you a bill that rivals the cost of the Korean War. Since you won't have a final drink tally until the end of the night, how much money should you allocate in your budget for booze? Here's a helpful formula that should get you pretty close.

Open-Bar-Alcohol-Budget Formula

Total booze bill =

$40 × number of people who are coming to the wedding

+

an extra $35 for each relative who drinks incessantly at family events because of a host of psychological issues that will probably never be resolved

+

an extra $400 for that one crazy guy you were allowed to invite (let's hope he's worth it)

If you're still concerned about the cost of the booze, there are a few tricks you can use to mitigate the expense. For example, you can have an open bar for only part of the night. If you do this, though, be sure that nothing important is planned during the five minutes before the open bar shuts down. There's nothing worse than 97 percent of the guests missing the bride's dance with her father because they're trying to grab two more gimlets before time runs out.

You can also give people drink tickets, although this instantly creates a black market. Those who don't drink will start scalping their tickets to the highest bidder.

Alternatively, some caterers let you supply your own alcohol, which means you go to the liquor store and buy enough booze to warrant a telephone call from the store owner to the

Bureau of Alcohol, Tobacco & Firearms. In this scenario, the problem isn't cost but quantity. You're buying all your beer, wine, champagne, and liquor ahead of time. You want to get enough alcohol to last through the night but not so much that you have extra and spend the first decade of your marriage with a blood alcohol level that would embarrass Jim Beam himself. Here are some additional useful formulas to help you estimate the quantities you'll need to buy.

Supplying-Your-Own-Booze Quantity Formulas

BEER

Number of six-packs =

2 × number of guys at your wedding who'll be wearing baseball caps

+

3 × number of guys who will say, "I can't believe you're getting married during the playoffs!"

+

4 × number of people in the band

RED WINE

Number of bottles of cabernet =

number of guests who are having the steak for dinner

−

number of guests who have no idea what cabernet means

WHITE WINE

Number of bottles of chardonnay =

.5 × number of guests at your wedding

+

2 × number of women over forty who say: "I never drink, but tonight I'll just have a little chardonnay! One glass. That's it!"

THE BUBBLY

Number of bottles of champagne =

.5 × number of guests

+

one additional bottle to smash over the head of each person who says: "Technically, champagne must come from the Champagne region of France. This is a sparkling white wine."

LIQUOR

Number of bottles of liquor =

.25 × number of guests who are over eighteen

+

2.25 × number of guests who are under eighteen

+

3 × number of years groom's dad was in the army

+

10 × number of army buddies that groom's dad has invited

No matter how you wind up acquiring and paying for your booze, your view of alcohol will never be the same after your wedding. It would be nice if this change of view occurred because you learned some valuable lesson about drinking in excess and social responsibility. Instead, you have simply discovered that your friends are wasteful with alcohol when you are paying for it and that totally pisses you off.

A buddy will grab a gin and tonic off a waiter's tray, have one sip, put the glass down, and head to the bathroom. When he comes back, he takes a *new gin and tonic* off the waiter's tray even though his old gin and tonic is still sitting there. Across the room, you see this go down, and even though it's the greatest night of your entire life, there's a small part of your brain that's thinking, Those gin and tonics are fourteen dollars a pop, jackass.

For the rest of your life, you will never put down a drink at another person's wedding until the glass is licked clean. You'll take your drink into the bathroom. You'll finish other people's drinks. You'll get a doggy bag for your martini at the end of the night. While most of the guests will look at you like you're crazy, the host will come up to you at the end of the night and say, "From now on, you're my only real friend."

Setting the Table

With the food and drink decisions settled, you've still got to decide how your guests will get this delicious meal into their mouths. "With their hands" may be the most accurate answer, but since some of your friends and business colleagues have (thankfully) never seen your family eat before, it's always nice to create the illusion of civility.

You'll need to pick out a full table setting: tablecloth, napkins, dishes, glasses, and utensils. A few of the choices will be fairly straightforward. For example, when it comes to the dinner plates, your options are (a) the ones that are included with the cost of the food and (b) the ones that are clean.

Most of the choices, however, are more complicated. The tablecloth is a good example. The caterer will tell you that he can do white, ivory, or black. Or, if your bride wants a challenge, the caterer also has a book of three thousand different fabric colors that he can special order. Your bride chooses ivory and you head home. Moments later, you wake up from your daydream and realize that you're still at the caterer's office and that your fiancée is buried in the book of special fabric colors.

The bride eventually brings the book home, and she and her friends stay up until three in the morning looking at the book. You tell your bride that she needs to get more sleep. She's not in college anymore! She agrees and says she's done with the tablecloths. The napkins, however...

Knock Her Socks Off

There are lots of little things you can do to keep the alcohol bill from spiraling out of control. People want to drink at weddings, but they'll also tend to drink whatever you serve them. So pick a reasonably priced wine that you think tastes good and have waiters come around with prepoured glasses during the cocktail hour. Most of your guests will gladly have the wine instead of waiting in line at the bar for more expensive cocktails.

The same logic can be applied to the booze. You don't have to serve every spirit that's available on the market. For each type of liquor, pick an inexpensive brand to use in mixed drinks ("inexpensive brand" means that it has a name you've never heard of and is sold at places that also sell handguns) and a higher-quality brand to serve to the connoisseurs ("higher quality" means that it is not in a plastic bottle).

For the Bride

The food is an area of wedding planning where the groom will be very knowledgeable and helpful. Unlike designing an invitation or arranging a centerpiece, the groom has occasionally eaten dinner in his life and therefore has some experience he can draw upon.

Ladies, please enjoy this momentous occasion. Your fiancé is actually offering useful information. It's a great moment. And then the moment will be ruined when you ask your groom what type of plates he thinks you should use and he says, "Paper!"

15

So, Basically Your Dress Costs a Thousand Dollars an Hour, Right?

Getting Your Outfits for the Big Day

When it comes to selecting the appropriate wedding attire, you'll probably notice a big difference in the way you and your bride will go about getting your outfits for the occasion. What follows is an itemized comparison.

Bride

1. Visits every bridal salon within two-hundred-mile radius of her home.

2. Returns to every bridal salon with her mother.

3. Has fight with her mother.

4. Returns to every bridal salon with friends and talks about how crazy her mother is.

5. Selects dress and puts down a deposit.

6. Decides that she hates the dress. Puts down deposit on another dress.

7. Has another fight with mother, who liked the first dress.

8. Cancels second dress and goes back to first dress just to get her mother off her back.

9. Bride's mother sees a third dress on sale and recommends it.

10. Bride has a breakdown because she's already ordered two dresses and now her mom wants her to consider a third?!

11. Bride sees the third dress and falls in love with it.

12. Bride orders the third dress.

13. Bride reconciles with her mother.

14. Bride and her mother cry tears of joy over this glorious event.

Groom

1. Get tux.

2. Eat burger.

3. Nap.

To Rent or Not to Rent, That Is the Question

The issue of whether to rent or buy your outfit applies only to you, the groom. Your bride would rather be trapped in a crowded elevator for three years than wear a rented wedding dress. Even if she's short on cash, making a dress, borrowing a dress, or going naked are all preferable to renting. Acquiring a tuxedo, however, is more complicated.

Reasons to Rent Your Tuxedo	Reasons to Buy Your Tuxedo
Cheaper.	When you tell the salesclerk your size, he'll actually listen.
Less expensive.	It feels cool and sophisticated to own a tux.
It doesn't cost as much money.	Your tux will be composed of something other than polyester and starch.
Of the two options, this one requires you to withdraw fewer dollars from your bank account.	Your tuxedo won't smell like someone else's back sweat.
There may be a price difference between renting and buying that favors the renting option.	Your tuxedo will have been made after 1974.

Whatever you decide to do with regards to a tuxedo (by the way, renting is cheaper), you'll soon be faced with a variety of attire decisions. There is one guiding principle you should use when making your selections:

Guiding Principle You Should Use
When Selecting Your Outfit

Resist the temptation to dress like a clown.

No one knows why pink tuxedo jackets exist, but it isn't your responsibility to find out. Most salesclerks are decent people who will remind you of this. However, you may run into the occasional person who is trying to clear out his inventory and views your body as the perfect Dumpster.

You can tell what sort of salesclerk you are dealing with by what components of the tuxedo he recommends you acquire.

GREEN LIGHT: WHAT A GOOD SALESPERSON RECOMMENDS YOU GET

- Black tuxedo jacket

- Black tuxedo pants

- Tuxedo shirt

- Studs and cuff links for the shirt

- Bow tie

- Cummerbund or vest

- Black shoes

**YELLOW LIGHT: YOU MAY BE IN TROUBLE IF YOUR
SALESPERSON IS RECOMMENDING THESE ITEMS**

- A white tuxedo jacket (Some people can pull this off, but you're probably not one of them.)

- A monocle

- A Congressional Medal of Honor

- An English accent

**RED LIGHT: YOUR SALESPERSON HAS GONE OFF THE DEEP
END IF HE'S RECOMMENDING THIS STUFF**

- A tuxedo jacket in a fruit-flavor color

- Tear-away pants

- A vest that can also be used as a flotation device

If the tuxedo components seem too complicated, keep in mind that there are alternative attire options.

A NICE SUIT

Every guy looks great in a nice suit, although there will inevitably be disagreement about what sort of suits qualify as "nice." For most grooms, nice is synonymous with "already owned." Desperate guys may also claim that dry cleaning a bad suit will make it nice, as though somehow acknowledging the existence of dry cleaners shows their inherent sense of style. Your bride will remind you that a groom is qualified to judge suit quality only if his last name is also a store on Rodeo Drive.

So off you go to buy a suit. Since you were warned only about crazy tuxedo salesmen and not crazy suit salesmen, you return home an hour later looking like Mr. Peanut.

A SIMPLE BLACK SUIT

Always a good choice. Just don't wear a black necktie with your black suit or you'll look like you had a starring role in the film *Reservoir Dogs*.

A NAVY BLAZER, TROUSERS, AND A TIE

This distinguished and preppy look is always appropriate. It's best worn, however, when the wedding is taking place on the quarterdeck of your yacht.

BUSINESS CASUAL

This attire is acceptable only during Friday afternoons in the summer, and not if you're meeting with clients.

COWBOY

In order to wear this to your wedding you must either (a) be able to lasso a horse or (b) beat the Green Bay Packers this weekend.

TRADITIONAL SCOTTISH KILT

Even the most refined best man will come up to you during the reception and say, "Nice skirt."

The Bridal Party

Now that your outfit is in place, it's time to figure out what the groomsmen and bridesmaids will wear. You don't have to buy their outfits for them, but you'll need to tell them how they should dress. Not surprisingly, the issues confronting the bridesmaids' dresses are drastically different from those surrounding the groomsmen's attire.

Issue	Concern for Bridesmaids	Concern for Groomsmen
Color	What color flatters their figures?	What color hides red wine stains well?
Size	Is the dress available in a variety of sizes?	Are the guys aware that clothes *come* in a variety of sizes?
Cost	Will they have to spend more than three hundred dollars?	Will they have to spend more than three dollars?
Uniqueness	Do the dresses look too much like the ones your friend picked for her bridesmaids?	Do the tuxes look just like the one my friend wore at his wedding? They do? Perfect!
Shoes	Will they be able to walk in heels?	Will they think that white sneakers + black Sharpie = dress shoes?

Issue	Concern for Bridesmaids	Concern for Groomsmen
Accessories	Will they remember to wear the earrings I gave them?	Will they remember to wear pants?

There will be other challenges as well. For starters, no matter when your fiancée orders the bridesmaids' dresses, they will not arrive on time. She could have ordered the outfits when she was in fifth grade, and yet she'll still be on the phone with UPS three days before the wedding, wondering why the dresses are in Micronesia.

When the dresses finally do arrive, none of them will fit. This would be expected had the bridesmaids not gone in for a fitting before the dresses were ordered. Apparently, the fitting is done only to provide the illusion of organization. After the fittings are over, the dressmaker throws the measurements away. So, the night before the wedding all the bridesmaids head to The Gap and pick out a forty-five-dollar dress that most of them like better anyway.

The groomsmen can get their measurements at a tux shop and then leave with a rental on the same visit, which would seem to eliminate most problems. What you'll fail to take into account is that the groomsmen won't actually go to the tux store. Well, that's not entirely accurate. They do go to the tux store...at eight forty-two the night before your wedding. The store closes at five p.m. When you tell your groomsmen that this situation is unacceptable, they respond, unhelpfully, with: "I know, right!? What sort of tux store isn't open twenty-four hours a day?!" So, off the groomsmen go to The Gap to buy forty-five-dollar dresses that most of them like better anyway.

Wedding-Dress Primer

The only outfit that really matters, of course, is the bride's. Traditionally, the groom does not see the wedding dress until the day of the wedding. But he will certainly be aware of it. Not only does the bride have to show the dress to every female relative who passes through the county, but she also has to go in for a fitting every six days. Here's what happens at each of the fittings.

FITTING #1

Bride's measurements are taken.

FITTING #2

Bride's measurements are taken again because bride went home and did 4,732 sit-ups after her measurements were taken the first time.

FITTING #3

The dressmaker creates a facsimile of the gown out of a simple fabric like cotton or muslin. The bride tries on this mock-up dress and gets it tailored so that it fits her perfectly. Everything is flawless, which totally freaks the bride out because there's no way her dress can be this perfect. She goes home and thinks of ways to make the process more complicated.

FITTING #4

Bride comes in with a list of changes she wants made to the dress.

FITTING #5

Bride sees the dress with the changes she wanted and isn't sure she likes them. Bride says she wants to wear the cotton mock-up instead of the finished dress on her wedding day.

FITTING #6

Dressmaker quits the business.

FITTING #7

Bride convinces the dressmaker to come back to work.

FITTING #8

Bride tries on finished dress, and it's the most beautiful garment in the entire world. Everyone is thrilled. Then, as the bride is taking off the dress, it catches on her watch and rips in half.

Meanwhile, all of these fittings have a subliminal effect on the groom. You suddenly feel like you're neglecting your own outfit—your bride thinks about her dress every day and you haven't taken the tux out of the closet in weeks! As a solution, you decide to start wearing your tux around the house, thus ensuring that when the actual day of the wedding rolls around, there'll be a nice soy sauce stain on your shirt for everyone to see.

Knock Her Socks Off

There's an old saying that a bride needs to wear something old, something new, something borrowed, and something blue on her wedding day. Mercifully, there isn't a similar rule for grooms, since that would just confuse us.

One of the nice parts about the bride's tradition, though, is the idea of wearing something old. Oftentimes, this is a piece of jewelry that belonged to a family member. Although not required, it can be really nice for the groom to observe this practice as well. Even if the men in your family aren't big jewelry wearers, you can still probably wrestle up a pair of cuff links from your grandfather or a watch from your dad (or a nipple ring from your brother). Whatever you choose to wear, it will bring additional sentiment to your wedding-day outfit.

For the Bride

Ladies, when it comes to the cost of your dress, your man will say all the right things. He'll tell you that this is a once-in-a-lifetime event (he hopes!) and you should get the dress you want, cost be damned. However, when it comes time to tell him the actual cost of the dress, you should lie to him. Seriously. Everyone will be happier. Tell him a number that is *at least* 30 percent less than the actual cost of the dress. Marriage is based on being truthful and honest—except in this one case.

16

Honey, Is Our Love More Like a Gentle Snowfall or a Beautiful Sunset?

Creating Your Wedding Ceremony

Many couples may not have the option of customizing what they say during the wedding. For example, you may be having a religious ceremony in which all of the language is predetermined. Or, alternatively, you may be standing in a Vegas wedding chapel at three in the morning, too trashed to say anything except, "What's your name again?"

In many cases, however, there is at least some flexibility, which allows the bride and groom to determine the content of their wedding ceremony. If you have such power, embrace it. Your guests will view the ceremony as one of the most important parts of the wedding day, behind only the food, the booze, the music, the flowers, the other people in attendance, how much they're paying for their hotel room, how much they spent on your wedding present, and tomorrow's weather.

Part 1: The Vows

The most important part of any wedding ceremony is the vows you and your bride will exchange. You know you'll be saying "I do," but you have to decide what you're actually agreeing *to* do.

A lot of couples like to take the creative route. The bride and groom go off separately and come up with a list of promises that they will make to each other at the altar. The bride and groom keep these promises secret until they read them aloud during the ceremony. This is a lovely idea. The problem is that, often, one of you will come up with very romantic promises and the other one will come up with very practical promises. When taken together, the vows sound, well, uneven:

> BRIDE: I promise that I will respect you and love you every day of my life.

> GROOM: I promise not to roll my eyes when you tell me to turn off the game because we're running late and really have to leave right now.

> BRIDE: I promise to be a pillar of support that you can always lean on when times get tough.

> GROOM: I promise that I'll try to remember to take out the garbage because I know how pissy you get when I don't.

Another option is to use vows that you've heard and liked at other people's weddings. There will be no surprises—you'll each have signed off on what the other one is saying. You have to be careful, however, that you've tweaked the language so that it's appropriate for the two of you.

Vow	You Should Probably Tweak the Vow if...
"Every hair on my body tingles with excitement when you walk into the room."	the groom is bald.
"You mean more to me than anyone else on Earth."	this is the groom's fifth marriage, and his many children are sitting in the first row.
"I'll love you until the day I die."	you are both over ninety.
"My heart skips a beat when I see you."	the groom had bypass surgery shortly after meeting the bride.
"We'll never be apart."	the bride is participating in the wedding via teleconference machine.

You also want to make sure that the people whose vows you are borrowing are *not* in attendance at your wedding. Couples feel as though their particular vows are sacred and can't be used by anyone else, even if all they said to each other was "I love you." So be careful, because if you also say, "I love you," expect someone in the second row to stand up and yell, "Find something original to say, you vow pirate!"

As a third and final option, you can just use the universal vow, which follows. When you come to a phrase in parentheses, simply choose the option that is the most appropriate for your relationship.

Universal Wedding Vow
(Can Be Said by Either Bride or Groom)

Darling, today is the (luckiest/happiest) day of my life. Why? Because I'm marrying you, and you're (terrific/ amazing/wonderful). Our love is like (waves crashing on the beach/the stars in the sky) and I really believe we are (meant for each other/soul mates/two of a kind).

I still remember the first time I saw you. You were (sitting across the bar from me/dating my best friend/up for parole). Our first date to (the movies/that burger place/a cheap motel) was such magic that I knew I wanted to be with you (for all eternity/until we had slept together). I promise this day that I'll never (leave your side/ask you to role-play in bed). Thank you for loving me, and you know I'll always (love you back/ask you to role-play in bed even though I just said I wouldn't).

Part 2: The Officiant's Words

The officiant will likely want to meet with the two of you at least once before the wedding. At this meeting, he will ask each of you a series of questions, in hopes that he will get to know you better and can thus speak more truthfully about your relationship during the ceremony. The officiant's questions are meant to be thought provoking and introspective, and the list often includes some of the following:

- Pick three adjectives that you think describe the other person.

- Tell me about the moment in the relationship that you're most proud of.

- If you could change one thing about how you treat the other person, what would it be?

- If each of you were a type of vegetable, what do you think you'd be?

The two of you quickly ignore the first three questions (bor-ring!) and have an enthusiastic discussion about what type of vegetable you would be. Your fiancée thinks she's truffles, because she's rare and special! You think you're an artichoke because you're hard on the outside and soft and fuzzy in the center. You then begin assigning vegetable personalities to all of your friends ("Steve is *such* an eggplant!") and soon have a spirited debate as to whether sugar beets are a fruit or a vegetable.

Though it may be hard to pull yourself away from the vegetable analogies (it's a slippery slope), you and your bride should also use this time to learn more about the officiant. You'll need to decide whether you're going to write out, verbatim, what you want the officiant to say, or whether you'll just give him an outline and trust his judgment. To decide what path to take, it's now your turn to ask the officiant some questions.

The Officiant Quiz

1. We'd like our ceremony to be around thirty minutes long. Which of the following do you most associate with a length of thirty minutes?
   a. An episode of *Seinfeld*
   b. The film *Lawrence of Arabia*
   c. The Hundred Years War
   d. The Paleozoic Era

2. Which of the following topics do you think is appropriate to discuss during our wedding?
   a. Bubonic plague
   b. Abortion
   c. Gun control
   d. Waterfalls

3. What are our first names?
   a. Nick and Francesca
   b. Danny and Danni
   c. John and Yoko
   d. Why should I give a crap about your first names?

4. How did we meet?
   a. Set up by some mutual friends.
   b. Bride was groom's divorce lawyer for his first marriage.
   c. Bride was groom's mistress throughout his first marriage.
   d. We haven't really "met," we just had anonymous sex and now she's pregnant.

5. How many weddings have you performed?
    a. Dozens
    b. This is only my second wedding, but I've done hundreds of divorces.
    c. Are we only counting legal weddings?
    d. You want me to actually marry you? I thought I was just reading a Robert Frost poem.

If the officiant gives an unsatisfactory answer to any of these questions, you should be sure and write out the ceremony in its entirety for him to read. If he gets all five of the questions wrong, you should fire him and revert back to using your actor friend who wants to get ordained on the Internet. (Although he's now decided that a Christopher Walken voice would be much funnier than Sean Connery's.)

Part 3: The Readings

Having your friends and relatives perform readings during the wedding can be very memorable and special. It also help break up the ceremony, serving as sort of a commercial break before the big finale: "Barbara and Gary are finally going to exchange rings...but before they do, please enjoy these fine words from Aunt Molly."

The first thing you'll have to decide is who should perform these readings.

Person	Pro	Con
Grandparent	Sentimental choice.	"Where in the name of Franklin D. Roosevelt did I put my glasses?"
College roommate	Spirited personality.	Really wants to come to the wedding ceremony, but "not sure what else is going on that night."
Older brother	Loving family member.	Gives you a noogie on his way to the podium.
Parents	Most influential people in your life.	Unenthusiastic because they're convinced that reading a poem will somehow make the wedding more expensive.
Rev. Jesse Jackson	Inspirational.	After the ceremony, the guests have no interest in the bride and groom— they just wander around the reception proudly saying, "Well, when I was talking to Jesse earlier . . ."

You'll then make the mistake of assuming that the texts these people read aloud are actually important. They're not. The only thing that matters is their length. Anything sounds great if it takes less than two minutes to recite. Your grandpa can read a parking ticket aloud, and if it only takes ninety seconds, people will smile from ear to ear. By contrast, you could have a story that Ernest Hemingway himself penned for you, but after the first paragraph, your guests will be far more interested in staring at their knuckles than hearing about how your love is like a Spanish bullfight.

If one of your readers begins to ramble and it's getting uncomfortable, there are several things you can do. First, you can take a page out of the Academy Awards and have your musicians start playing a soft tune—the audience claps, the reader gets the hint, and you move on to the next item. If that doesn't work, you can always signal the sound guy to cut the microphone at the podium. You and your bride say there must be a technical problem, and the reader leaves the stage confused. If none of those solutions work, you can simply supply your audience with rotten tomatoes and give your officiant a gigantic vaudeville hook.

Whoever you have do the readings, be sure that he or she sits near the front of the ceremony. If it takes too long for Uncle Vic to make his way to the podium, some person in the audience will grow restless and start to boo. The rest of the crowd will notice the heckler is booing an elderly man, so they'll start booing the heckler. And suddenly your wedding has turned into amateur night at the Roxy.

Part 4: The Rest of the Ceremony

Although you've now got the major stuff covered, there are other parts of the ceremony that also need to be written out. These include the welcome from the officiant, the explanation of any religious customs that you are observing, and the presentation of the married couple at the end of the ceremony.

While these elements are indeed important, you and your bride will probably forget to write them. You're busy working on your vows and dodging calls from people who want to do readings, so the rest of the ceremony slips your mind. As a result, your officiant is forced to wing it the day of the marriage. His welcome consists of: "Right. Let's do this thing." The explanation of religious customs winds up being: "The lighting of the candle and the drinking of wine is really important. I can't tell you why. Just trust me. It's important." And the presentation of the married couple is: "Kiss her, man, 'cause I need a bourbon."

The Marriage License

All the effort you've put into creating your ceremony and writing your vows won't mean a thing if you don't have a marriage license. The cruel truth is that the moment you and your bride are legally married does not occur during the ceremony. It happens weeks later, deep in the bowels of a government building when the proper paperwork is filed and recorded.

Although the actual process varies by state and county, the basic idea is that you go get a marriage license before the ceremony, then you fill it out and sign it after the wedding. Afterward, you return the license to the proper government agency, and once it's processed, you're married. No problem, right? Well...

MARRIAGE LICENSE PROBLEM #1: THE HOURS

First you discover that your county issues marriage licenses only on Thursday afternoons from two forty-five until two forty-eight. It takes several weeks of trying until you finally arrive at the correct time.

MARRIAGE LICENSE PROBLEM #2: ELIGIBILITY

It turns out that since your fiancée was born in Canada and never became a U.S. citizen, there are all sorts of problems getting the license. You explain that Canada and America have a lot in common, like the NHL, but that doesn't seem to do the trick.

MARRIAGE LICENSE PROBLEM #3: YOUR OFFICIANT

Freedom of religion is one of the cornerstones of our democracy, so if your officiant is a member of a recognized religious group, you should have no problem. Your friend Gary who is performing the ceremony, however, neglected to mention that he was a devout follower of the Church of the New York Mets.

The good news is that your county government will probably have a solution to all your problems. Just down the hall from the marriage license office, there's a place where your fiancée can get naturalized. Three doors down from that office you can have a civil ceremony performed by a legitimate officiant. It's the government's version of a shopping mall, and, frankly, you might sort of like it. If they put in a Barnes & Noble and a food court, you'd probably go there on weekends.

Knock Her Socks Off

You've spent all this time and energy putting together your ceremony, so be sure everyone can hear it. Rent a microphone. Most people assume that if they are having an indoor wedding or a fairly intimate outdoor wedding they don't need a microphone. Why take chances? Even if you, your bride, and the officiant have booming voices, you're not going to want to be shouting at each other for forty-five minutes.

For the Bride

If your groom is standing at the altar next to you, it's safe to assume that he's madly in love with you and wants to be with you forever. So don't make him say a vow that he's uncomfortable with just because you like the sound of it. "We will run through a field of poppies together, skipping and laughing as the sweet floral aroma fills the air and our souls" is gonna freak some guys out. If your man doesn't want to say he loves you, that's a big problem. If your man doesn't want to sound like an eight-year-old Swiss girl while reciting his vows, cut him some slack.

17

Why Is Vomiting a Prerequisite to Marriage?

The Highs and Lows of the Bachelor Party

Bachelor parties are supposed to be the groom's final chance to bid farewell to his crazy days of being single. However, most dudes were not that crazy when they were single and were not getting laid until they met their fiancée. Thus, were a bachelor party to accurately reflect what the man is giving up, he should probably stay home alone that weekend, order some Chinese food, and watch *Real Sex* on HBO. Since that's a somewhat depressing prospect, it's off to Las Vegas!

Upon arriving in Vegas, your best man will quickly assign everyone a role. It's very much like casting a play. It doesn't really matter which of your friends is playing which part, as long as every role is filled.

Bachelor Party Dramatis Personae

Role	Description
The Crazy Guy	Tries hard to get you kicked out of the casino and/or into a street fight with a rival bachelor party.
The Compulsive Gambler	Remains at the blackjack table the entire weekend; is still there when your wedding day eventually rolls around.
The Dorky Guy	Keeps asking when you're going on the tour of the Hoover Dam.
The Guy Who Takes Off and Is Never Seen Again	Vanishes immediately to an unknown destination; resurfaces as you are boarding the plane to leave Vegas.
The Guy with Young Kids	Just psyched to do anything that doesn't involve poopy diapers.
The Guy You're Not Really Friends with Anymore but Who's Still Invited	Creates awkward tension by continually saying, "Back when I saw you more often . . ."
The Vaguely European Guy	Goes around claiming he can "totally hook us up in Vegas." As a result, you find yourself in a dance club at three in the morning paying seventy-two dollars for a Bud Light in a city famous for its free drinks.

Once all the roles are cast, the best man will ask everyone to synchronize their watches because for the next day and a half, you'll be adhering to the strict Las Vegas bachelor-party timeline.

Strict Timeline for Las Vegas Bachelor Party

4:00 P.M.:	Group decides to do a little gambling.
4:01 P.M. to 4:11 P.M.:	While playing blackjack, every guy loses most of the money he's brought for the whole weekend.
4:12 P.M. to 5:00 P.M.:	Group switches to slots in an attempt to slow down losing.
5:01 P.M.:	Group has now lost the rest of their money playing slots.
5:00 P.M. to 6:00 P.M:	Group decides to take a walk along the strip.
6:01 P.M.:	Walk along strip results in group entering a new casino.
6:02 P.M.:	Group hits the ATM and resumes gambling in new casino.
6:47 P.M.:	One dude wins a lot of money, convincing everyone else that they will soon do the same.
7:30 P.M.:	Everyone is again out of money, including the dude who won a lot of money.
7:45 P.M.:	Group returns to the hotel to get ready for dinner; everyone agrees to meet at 8:30 p.m. to walk to the restaurant.

8:30 P.M.:	No one is at the assigned meeting place.
10:00 P.M.:	Final few people arrive at meeting place.
10:15 P.M. to 12:15 A.M.:	Most expensive dinner of all time; even if everyone is having only rye toast, bill still comes to $425 per person.
12:16 A.M. to 12:30 A.M.:	Group attempts to go to a strip club but winds up in a seedy neighborhood and is mugged. Luckily, no one has any money.
12:45 A.M. to 4:00 A.M.:	More gambling and drinking and rationalizing the cost of weekend. Everyone talks repeatedly about that one dude who won a lot of money at 6:47 p.m. as that dude maxes out his cash-advance limit on his credit card.
11:00 A.M.:	Group meets at breakfast buffet and has the grossest combination of foods ever conceived.

After the buffet is awkwardly digested, it's time to head home. Everyone is exhausted, broke, hungover, and nauseous. Yet, for the rest of time, whenever any dudes from the weekend see each other, they reminisce about how much money they won and how the breakfast buffet was totally delicious. Selective and inaccurate memories—where would we be without them?

Alternative Locations

Although Vegas is a popular choice, not all grooms like the idea of losing all their money and getting beat up by casino goons (although, for the life of me, I can't figure out why).

For those looking for an alternative way to celebrate the end of their bachelor days, there are a plethora of options.

MEXICO

It's sunny. It's warm. It's inexpensive. However, there are not enough laws prohibiting things that you'll later regret doing.

RENT A HOUSE

For guys who prefer a mellow evening, renting a house on a lake or in the woods allows for plenty of eating, drinking, merriment, and memories. Unfortunately, it also sounds like the setting for a Stephen King novel.

THE LOCAL PARTY

The groom and his buddies rent a limo and cruise around the city, barhopping and howling at the moon. It's simple, fun, and easy to arrange. On the downside, the groom manages to run into his boss, the bride's parents, his ex-girlfriend, and his wedding planner over the course of the evening.

THE I'M-NOT-HAVING-A-BACHELOR-PARTY BACHELOR PARTY

The groom declares he doesn't want to have a bachelor party, but then, the weekend before the wedding, he begins to have regrets. His friends scramble to put something together at the last minute, which generally involves a depressing outing to the liquor store and/or Blockbuster video.

SIOUX CITY, IOWA

What? You could have fun in Sioux City, Iowa. I think. Maybe.

The Aftermath

No matter where you go and what you end up doing, the final day of the bachelor party resembles a procedural crime drama. The disoriented groom examines the evidence in front of him and must slowly piece together the events of the weekend.

For example, you wake up on Sunday morning and notice that your knee is bleeding, you're handcuffed to a goat, and your wallet is missing. On closer inspection, you see that there are several small gashes on your knee and bits of rusty metal stuck in your pants. The handcuffs are standard police issue. The goat is named Sally, which is also the name of your fiancée. And your wallet isn't missing—it's lying beside you, with all the cash gone.

How did you get to this moment? It's now pretty obvious what went down. While drunk, you climbed a barbed-wire fence because one of your buddies heard that a goat on the other side of the fence had the same name as your fiancée and wanted to get a picture. But the farmer who owned the goat heard your screams when you cut your knee on the barbed wire. The farmer quickly called the police. When the cops arrived, they decided to teach you a lesson, so they handcuffed you to the goat. Your friends then bribed the cops to go away, using the money in your wallet. That's really the only logical explanation for what happened.

With the mystery solved and the weekend winding down, the groom now faces a critical decision: Do I tell my fiancée what happened? The answer is yes. You need to establish trust with your new partner, and this is the perfect opportunity to show her that there are no secrets between you. Also, she won't believe a word you say. She'll assume (incorrectly) that you weren't stupid enough to climb a barbed-wire fence because someone saw a goat named Sally. It's the best of both worlds—you've told the truth and your fiancée isn't mad. Now if only you could find the keys to those handcuffs.

The Caveat

The one exception to all these bachelor party scenarios happens when the last person in your group of friends gets married. Most guys tie the knot in their late twenties and early thirties, but there's always the one dude who waits until he's forty-four. All the guys return to Vegas for one last hurrah, but soon realize they are no longer twenty-five years old. They have wives. And kids. And careers. And high blood pressure. What all the guys really want to do is get a massage to ease their lumbar pain, eat a low-cholesterol dinner, and stay in a hotel that has sheets with a high thread count. So that's exactly what happens, and it's the single best weekend ever.

Knock Her Socks Off

For the record, you are not a huge dork if you *don't* feel the need to have a crazy bachelor party weekend. If that's the case, a nice alternative can be a joint bachelor-bachelorette party with your bride. Joint parties can be whatever you want: a beach weekend away with friends, karaoke night, wine tasting, a cocktail party. In fact, just about anything will work, as long as it doesn't involve you sitting home alone on a Saturday night and watching *Real Sex.*

For the Bride

Ladies, only you know the real secret: Your bachelorette party was less costly, more fun, and much crazier than your fiancé's bachelor party. While your groom was casually playing blackjack and sipping a beer at two a.m., you were standing on the bar at the Cowboy Club, whipping your shirt in the air and singing along to the jukebox that was blasting "I Hate Myself for Loving You" by Joan Jett.

You should feel free to tell your man what went down at the bachelorette party. He'll think you're lying, because "no one parties as hard as my friends" and "we had the wildest weekend ever." Therefore, both of you enter the marriage having been completely honest with each other *and* in a state of ignorant bliss. You think he's actually much smarter than he is, and he thinks you're actually more conservative than you really are. And that translates into decades of happy marriage!

18

Is There Any Money Left for a Honeymoon?

Planning a Much-Needed Vacation

The first decision you'll be faced with when planning the honeymoon is whether to go right after the wedding or to wait awhile and go at some point down the road. In many ways, waiting is the more logical option. You're already way behind at your job; a trip in the future gives you something to look forward to so you can avoid a postwedding letdown; you can start saving money again and take a nicer, more expensive trip in a few months or years.

On the downside, if you take a vacation in the future, you won't really be honeymooning. Instead, you'll be a married couple on vacation. And there are some key differences between a honeymooning couple and a married couple on vacation.

Problem	Honeymooning Couple Says	Married Couple on Vacation Says
The hotel room has a tiny bed.	"Let's pretend we're in college!"	"Let's get two rooms."
You get lost in your rental car.	"It's a fun adventure!"	"Let's sue Avis for making this inaccurate map."
Inclement weather.	"Rain is romantic."	"Don't give me that 'rain is romantic' garbage."
You lose your cell phone.	"I've been meaning to get a new one anyway."	"No cell phone?! Does this mean we actually have to talk to each other?"
A waiter at a restaurant over-charges you for a bottle of wine.	"We'll just ask the waiter to redo the check."	"Let's pay the extra money so we can complain about the restaurant for the rest of the trip."
Museum you wanted to visit is closed for repairs.	"We'll come back in a few years and see it then."	"Guess I'll die without ever seeing the Mona Lisa."
You forgot birth control.	"Let's buy condoms."	"Let's not kid ourselves."

It's thus clearly best to go away right after the wedding if you can. The good news is that because this trip is your honeymoon, wherever you go will be special. The bad news is that the previous statement is untrue. You don't want to start your marriage in total conflict with each other because the truck stop where you're honeymooning at has, shockingly, turned out to be sort of crappy. It's still best to consider some of the more traditional options.

FLORIDA

It's sunny, it's warm, and it's easy to get to. But look who stopped by for breakfast—it's Grandma and Grandpa!

EUROPE

It's a continent rich in history, culture, and world-famous sites. On the downside, it tends to be a bit more expensive than Florida, although you can usually go on the Internet and find great airfare deals...to Estonia.

AFRICAN SAFARI

You spend the entire day watching an elephant have sex. You just don't need that sort of pressure when you return to your bedroom at night.

AUSTRALIA

Koalas? Kangaroos? Nicole Kidman? Sign me up! Just be sure you budget thirty-three days to get there.

SKIING IN THE ROCKY MOUNTAINS

You've always wanted to do this. It should be breath-takingly beautiful and definitely get the blood pumping. On the flip side...are you kidding me?! What sort of couple needs to get their blood pumping *after* planning a wedding?!

SOMEWHERE NEARBY

This is just a fancy way of saying you're having sex on the futon in the apartment above your neighbor's garage.

Once you decide where you're going and lock in your plans, everyone you know will then try to give you ideas for how you can make your honeymoon less relaxing. Many people will have been to the place you are going, but not for their honeymoon. They went to Venice with their church group or to Hawaii on their family vacation or to Miami on business. While each of these was no doubt a lovely trip, the overall motif was to be as busy as possible and return home exhausted. It seems obvious that you and your fiancée have a different agenda for your honeymoon, but that's irrelevant.

If you're going to Venice, for example, someone will say, "Here's a list of my ninety-four favorite duomos, and you should really see them all during the four days you are there. And you should go to Milan, Padua, Turin, and Bologna, too."

Additionally, people may even try to convince you to change your destination and plan a trip somewhere else: "I know there was a military coup in Chile last week, but it should still be at the top of your list."

Eventually, you just tell everyone that you're going to have sex on the futon in the apartment above your neighbor's garage, because no one else has done that and therefore can't offer you advice. Or, if they have done it, they're too embarrassed to talk about it.

The All-Inclusive Resort

Many couples opt for a warm-weather beach vacation because it provides slow-paced relaxation after the chaos of the wedding. In fact, this choice is so popular that tropical resorts often offer an all-inclusive honeymoon package. For a flat rate you and your new wife get:

1. Airfare on an airline you've never heard of

2. Seven nights' accommodation in a hotel room with a bed that twenty-three other couples have had sex on in the past month

3. Fourteen consecutive meals that feature chicken teriyaki

4. All the booze you can drink

Item 4 is the only one you really care about, so you quickly sign on the dotted line.

When you arrive at the resort, however, they have no record of your room reservation. "That's impossible!" you say. "I booked this trip on a travel Web site that's now out of business! How can there be any problem?!" The hotel manager is very apologetic and explains that the place is completely booked up with reservations that other couples made on different Internet travel sites that were probably just as sketchy but somehow *didn't* go out of business (yet).

Thankfully, the hotel manager has a solution. The hotel has a sister property on the other side of the island. This other hotel is more run-down, located in a swamp, and twice as expensive. Amazingly, they have a room available! The hotel manager assures you, though, that the sister property (a) still has the all-the-booze-you-can-drink policy and (b) does not require you to do a seating chart, pick out flowers, pose for photographs, engrave invitations, or interact with anyone you know... and that's music to your ears.

You check into your mediocre room at the sister property (which has a lovely view of a local political uprising that's taking place) and immediately lock the door so that you and your bride can begin a seventy-two-hour round-robin session of sex, sleep, and room service. Finally, you emerge from the room like a couple of grizzly bears coming out of hibernation—you're excited to get some sunshine, grab some food, and maybe maul a stupid tourist.

Once you get out and about at the resort, you're likely to meet other couples who are also there on their honeymoon. The couples will fall into one of the following categories:

Type of Couple You Meet on Your Honeymoon	What They Do
The couple that probably shouldn't have gotten married.	Discuss what they'll do differently during their next wedding.
The competitive couple.	Keep asking about details of your wedding in hopes that theirs was fancier.
The couple that was trying to book the wedding venue on the same night as you.	Eye you angrily from across the lobby.

Type of Couple You Meet on Your Honeymoon	What They Do
The couple that weirdly wants to be your best friends.	Phone you at dawn to ask if you want to go snorkeling yet again.
The couple that you think you know but really don't.	Assure you that their names aren't Bob and Shirley and that you didn't go to college with them.
The gross couple.	Lick each other while poolside.
The sexually open couple.	Continually ask for your room number.

Early in the honeymoon, you avoid all these couples because the two of you just want to be alone and relax. Then, as the week wears on, you and your wife make the transition from honeymooners to married couple on vacation, and realize that you don't need to be alone together twenty-four hours a day. Luckily, the other couples feel the same way, and you all quickly strike up a conversation about who's been solicited by the sexually open couple. Friendship ensues.

After the Honeymoon

In the days after you return from the honeymoon, there are some loose ends from the wedding that you'll need to address.

Post-Honeymoon To-Do List

1. Pick up wedding presents from your friends who have been receiving your packages while you were away.

2. Try to figure out how many of your gifts your friends have stolen and kept for themselves.

3. Begin writing thank-you notes.

4. Gain back the weight that you both lost for the wedding.

5. Write more thank-you notes.

6. Field calls from relatives asking why you haven't had children yet.

7. Have first official fight as a married couple (over the thank-you notes).

8. Open up wedding reply cards that are still trickling in three weeks after the event.

9. Kiss and make up over thank-you note fight.

10. Write more thank-you notes.

As noted, the majority of time between the end of your honeymoon and your seventieth birthday will be spent writing thank-you notes. The difficult aspect of thank-you notes isn't so much the quantity of notes you have to write, but rather the mind-numbing repetitiveness. To make it easier, I've provided a few handy templates that can be copied as often as needed.

Handy Thank-You Note Templates

EXAMPLE A: FOR A FRIEND OF YOUR PARENTS

Dear Mr. and Mrs. [last name]:

Thank you for [gift]. We love it! It was great to finally meet you after hearing my dad talk so often about your [distinguishing characteristic]. We look forward to seeing you at [name of upcoming event] in [month] and good luck with [name of their child]'s upcoming [wedding/bat mitzvah/plastic surgery]!

> Sincerely,
> [your name]

P.S. I'm [name of your father]'s kid, in case you have no idea who I am, even though you were at my wedding.

EXAMPLE B: FOR A FAMILY MEMBER

Dear [type of relation]:

First off, I absolutely adore [name of new spouse]—I mean, you'd never know that he/she [horrible thing about new spouse]. I'm so glad you decided to go off the registry and get us [weird gift], because we really love [awkward attempt on your part to make weird gift sound useful]. Let's promise to see each other again before another [multiple of ten] years go by.

> Sincerely,

[nickname you haven't used in twenty years but relative insists on using]

P.S. I'll be sure to give you a call if I'm ever in [most random location in America]!

EXAMPLE C: FOR A FRIEND OF YOURS

Dear [embarrassing nickname from college]:

How did you know I wanted [name of cheapest gift on your registry]?! I'm so thankful you could get time off from your work as a [name of temp job] to come celebrate with us! By the way, if you want [name of person at wedding your friend was drunkenly trying to hook up with]'s e-mail, I'll be happy to give it to you. Also, doesn't [name of mutual friend] look really hot now? And can you believe [name of other mutual friend] is gay?!

Sincerely,

Your Friend Who Once

[really awesome thing you did one time]

Knock Her Socks Off

When you're planning your trip, be sure to let the hotel know that you're on your honeymoon. Some places won't really care, but most will try to do something special for you—a nice room, a bottle of champagne, and lots of privacy.

While a bit more expensive, it can also be nice to use a travel agent. Not only can a travel agent help you plan the trip, but there's also someone to call when you show up at the hotel and they have no record of your reservation. Not that such a scenario would ever happen with a travel Web site that's now out of business.

If you're taking a long trip, consider giving yourself an extra day or two after the wedding before you leave. That way you don't have to worry about all the prevacation stuff (packing, stopping the mail, etc.) in the chaotic days before the wedding.

For the Bride

For whatever reason, brides tend to be extremely concerned about the cost of the honeymoon. Fiscal responsibility is wise, but it seems inconsistent to worry about how much the taxi ride from the airport to the hotel will cost ("Forty-five dollars—are you crazy?!") while at the same time giving each bridesmaid a timeshare in Vail as a thank-you gift. Relax. You've already plunged yourselves into debt for the next decade, so you might as well get the nice hotel room.

19

Who Asked This Person to Speak?
The Rehearsal Dinner

Having finally made all of the painstaking decisions that surround your wedding, the rehearsal dinner gives you the opportunity to relive the stress all over again. It's like one of those reality show flashback clips: "Welcome back to the finale of *Who Wants to Marry a Panda?* Before we find out whether Ling-Ling is going to choose Stephanie or Jessica as his wife, let's first take a look back at this season and remember how we got here!"

Some of the (familiar) questions you'll have to revisit when planning the rehearsal dinner are:

- Where do we have it?

- Who gets to come?

- Who's paying for it?

- What are we serving for dinner?

- Who's sending out the invitations?

- Why are we fighting?

- When does the pain stop?

The Ceremony Rehearsal

Before you get to the actual dinner, however, you first must have the rehearsal for the ceremony. This rehearsal usually takes place during the afternoon on the day before the wedding. Its purpose is to allow all the people in the bridal party to memorize exactly what they are supposed to do so that they can be sure they completely mess it up twenty-four hours later.

When you arrive at your venue, you will immediately notice that it is not set up for your wedding. That's because your wedding isn't until tomorrow and the venue is hosting a different event tonight—a hands-on fundraiser for the county zoo—so there are wood chips on the floor, chimpanzees screaming, and a zebra pooping in the corner. The proprietor of the venue assures you that everything will be cleaned up by tomorrow night, although he has difficulty keeping a straight face as he says this.

Regardless, you decide to press on. You push the flamingos off the altar and line up for the processional...only to realize that two of the groomsmen, the maid of honor, all the grandparents, and the father of the bride are missing.

The two groomsmen were coming in from out of town. You had explained to them that since the wedding rehearsal started at four p.m., they were cutting it a little close by taking a flight that landed at three fifty-eight. They assured you it wouldn't be a problem. As of twenty minutes ago, their flight still hadn't taken off.

The maid of honor is back at the hotel because she just had a terrible phone conversation with her boyfriend, Art (who she was already miffed at because he didn't want to come along as her date this weekend). Though the maid of honor later rationalizes the phone conversation to your bride by suggesting that "you don't know Art like I do," your bride feels obligated to spend hours convincing the maid of honor to dump this jerk because men can be total assholes. Your bride then turns to you and quickly adds the "except for you, babe" caveat.

The grandparents, meanwhile, went to the wrong venue. You're getting married at the Pierpont Hotel. They went to the Winthrop Hotel because "the service at the Pierpont is terrible!" The bride's dad has been dispatched to find the grandparents.

The few of you who are present practice walking down the aisle. The groom's dad rolls his eyes and says, "Why are we practicing such a mundane activity?" He then promptly trips.

You attempt to pair up the bridesmaids and groomsmen, but none of the women wants to walk in with "that creepy, desperate-for-sex" friend of yours, so he has to walk in alone, which only serves to make him creepier and more desperate for sex.

The officiant has forgotten the binder with the ceremony in it and can't remember what he's supposed to say. There's no music or microphone or lighting, and since neither you nor your bride wants to reveal your secret vows until the following night, everyone decides that the rehearsal is a huge success and heads to dinner.

The Last Supper (Before the Wedding)

The group awaiting you when you arrive at the rehearsal dinner promises to be a curious subsection of the guest list. Traditionally, the rehearsal dinner is for the bridal party and out-of-town guests. In today's era of jet travel and stepsiblings, however, this rule is less easy to enforce. It needs to be modified if one of the following situations occurs.

SITUATION A: LOTS OF OUT-OF-TOWN GUESTS

Many brides and grooms no longer live in the same city where they grew up, which means out-of-town guests may outnumber local guests. The easiest way to deal with this situation is just to have a large rehearsal dinner and include everyone.

If you still want to keep the event small, you can have a lottery. On separate pieces of paper, write down the various geographical locations that all the out-of-town guests hail from. Put the pieces of paper into a hat, pick out one location, and let everyone from that city come to the rehearsal dinner. If you're on a tight budget, don't hesitate to fix the lottery. "And the winner is...Vancouver! What's that? My college roommate is the only person from that town? What are the odds of that happening?!"

SITUATION B: DESTINATION WEDDING

If you're getting married somewhere exotic, then everyone, including the bride and the groom, is an out-of-town guest. The polite thing to do is to include everyone at the rehearsal dinner. Many people will not attend, however. Why? Because they've shelled out all this money to get to Hawaii and now your wedding activities are really getting in the way of their vacation.

SITUATION C: THE LARGE, LOCAL FAMILY

Many brides still like to observe the tradition of getting married in their hometown. This means that many of the bride's current friends are out-of-town guests. Which means the rehearsal dinner will consist of these current friends, not her crazy, extended family. Which is why many brides still like to observe this tradition.

Whatever group is assembled, everyone will have a good time. Or rather, everyone will *start off* having a good time. You'll enjoy some food and drink, catch up with friends you haven't seen in a while, and bask in the excitement of your upcoming nuptials...then the toasts start.

Even this part of the evening begins favorably. You and your bride have asked certain people to speak because they are (a) sentimental favorites or (b) good speakers. You don't need to be good friends with these people—someone else's grandmother can give the inspirational speech and the maitre d' can give the funny speech. Everyone will cry and chuckle and have a good time. You and your bride will get up and tell a silly anecdote about your first date, and the night reaches its logical conclusion.

Then, suddenly, the drunkest person at the event stands up and says he wants to say a few words about the bride and groom. He barfs and passes out before anything happens, but the dam has burst. Now everyone wants to say something, under the guise that This is what the bride and groom want, even though the bride and groom are standing there saying, "In no way do we even remotely want this."

These are some of the people who feel motivated to make toasts:

Person Giving the Toast	What That Person Says
Dude who was at your bachelor party	"I didn't get a chance to tell this offensive story at the bachelor party, but I'm sure it's appropriate to tell now."
Your boss	"You've complained about your family before, and now I see why!"
An obscure friend of your uncle's whom you've never seen before	"It's just been so great watching you grow up!"
Bride's sister	"Last week, the bride told me she thinks this wedding is a terrible idea."
The wedding planner	"The bride and groom were *such* a pain in the ass while we were planning this thing!"

Person Giving the Toast	What That Person Says
An ex-girlfriend of the groom	"Not everyone knows that the groom has a tattoo in the shape of Texas on his inner thigh, but I sure do!"

The good news is that as your friendships are crumbling, you and your bride can amuse yourself by playing a fun gamed called What's the Worst Part of the Toasts? Is it:

1. the quantity?

2. the length?

3. the awkward delivery?

4. the embarrassing content?

What's great about the game is that every answer is usually correct.

You Come Bearing Gifts

Now that all your groomsmen have sufficiently ruined your weekend with their toasts, the traditional thing to do is to thank them for their service to you by presenting each of them with a gift. You must give a gift to all your grooms-men...even those whose "service" will involve showing up stoned at the wedding.

Guys don't exchange presents as often as women do, so if

you're having trouble picking out a gift, you may want to consider one of the following options.

TIE

If you're requiring all your groomsmen to wear the same tie during the wedding, it can be a nice gesture on your part to provide that piece of clothing. Not only will it save your groomsmen money, but you also won't have to worry about anyone wearing one of those T-shirts that has a tie printed on it.

CUFF LINKS

If you're having a black-tie wedding, this is another fashion accessory that you can give as a gift. Plus, your groomsmen can use the cuff links again after the wedding. Just as soon as they run out and buy expensive dress shirts with French cuffs. Yeah. That will happen.

WALLET

This is the classic male fashion accessory and a great gift. However, you'll need to listen to the there-isn't-any-money-in-here joke a minimum of forty times.

SUNGLASSES

A fun gift, especially if you're having an outdoor or beach wedding. On the downside, it will take your groomsmen about two minutes to lose the gift.

A NICE BOTTLE OF WINE

A great gift for the sophisticated man. Now, if only you knew some sophisticated men...

The Night Before

Once the evening finally winds down (mercifully), you and your bride face an important choice: Should we go through with the wedding?

Of course I'm just kidding. By now, you both know that you're madly in love and never want to be apart. Also, canceling the wedding would mean losing your deposit at the florist. Not gonna happen. The real choice you must make is: Should you spend the night before the wedding together?

The answer greatly depends on the personality and temperament of both you and your bride.

You Should Spend the Night Apart if

- you both enjoy quiet, solitary reflection.

- absence will make your hearts grow fonder, leading to an emotional and fulfilling reunion the next day.

- you have an appreciation of classic wedding traditions.

On the flip side...

You Should *Not* Spend the Night Apart if

- the groom is the sort of guy who'll make a last-ditch effort to have sex with the hot waitress at Chili's before he's married.

- when the bride sleeps in hotel rooms alone, she tends to stay up all night crying hysterically and saying things like "Why am I so lonely?!" even though the entire hotel is filled with people she knows.

If you do wind up spending the night apart, the bride usually stays in the bridal suite and the groom stays somewhere less expensive, like on a park bench. Grooms used to be given their own hotel rooms, but they couldn't be trusted to lay off the minibar.

No matter where you both end up sleeping, your bride will take a moment before the night ends to celebrate a tender prewedding ritual: the exchanging of gifts between the two of you. Your bride will have picked out something wonderful for you to use during the wedding—a camera, a new watch, etc. And you will have gotten her...nothing. No one told you about this tradition! Thinking fast, you announce that you wanted to wait and get her something special on the honeymoon, because you know the shopping will be wonderful where you're going. She looks at you oddly, because you're going to the Grand Canyon.

Knock Her Socks Off

All the folks at your rehearsal dinner are also going to be at your wedding the following night (unless you uninvite them after their toasts). So try to make the rehearsal dinner different from your wedding dinner. If one event is indoors, have the other one outdoors. If you're serving fish at one event, have meat at the other. The difference doesn't have to be drastic—just something to distinguish the two meals.

A word of warning: Many grooms try to take this idea too far. If you're having a black-tie wedding, paintball, while different, may not be the best rehearsal-dinner activity.

For the Bride

Ladies, no matter how awkward the toasts become, you must try to prevent your man from getting totally trashed (even though it seems justified and you're thinking about doing the same). You'll be doing him a big favor. Remember: Neither one of you is going to want to be hungover on your big day. You have the rest of your married lives for that.

20

How Come It's Raining and Does Anyone Know Where Grandma Went and Is It Normal to Feel Nauseous?
The Big Day Arrives!

There are two wedding-day guarantees:

1. It will be the most wonderful day of your life.

2. Stuff will go wrong.

The maid of honor will lose her dress the night before the ceremony. Your cousin was last seen in the hotel bar at three a.m. talking to a woman who was probably a hooker, and now no one can find him. The person who is performing the nuptials will refer to you as Charles during the ceremony, even though Charles is the name of your bride's first husband.

Truth be told, though, many brides and grooms don't actually remember the details of their wedding because it all goes by so fast. Knowing ahead of time how the day will unfold will better help you preserve a lot of those memories. To that end, here's an outline of what the big day will be like.

Part 1: Getting Ready

The wedding can be divided into four parts, and getting ready is just the first. What's amazing is how different this part of the day is for the bride and for the groom, even though they are (hopefully) preparing for the same event.

EIGHT HOURS BEFORE THE WEDDING

The bride wakes up in the bridal suite and begins her day as though she is the president of the United States. She puts on a robe and slippers and opens the door to her room, where the morning paper is waiting, along with a pot of coffee. She pours herself a cup and moves into the living room part of the suite, where her cabinet—all the bridesmaids, her mother, the wedding planner, and the U.S. attorney general—has assembled.

The bride gets a status report from all present—the bridesmaids inform her that she has a zit on her face but "no one can see it," even though they just did. Her mother informs her that six guests have bailed from the wedding at the last minute with such halfhearted excuses as dry scalp or tennis elbow.

The bride thanks everyone and puts the wedding planner in charge of solving all the problems. The bride stands up, and before leaving the room says, "We've got a big day today, people. And I'm counting on all of you. The American people are counting on you too." The bride walks away to shower and change. Everyone claps in approval.

The groom, by contrast, wakes up in his own bedroom. The only one there to greet him is the dog, who has commemorated the significance of the day by taking an early-morning pee on all the gifts that the groom brought home from the rehearsal dinner. The groom walks into the living room and discovers a leak in the roof. He slides the couch out of the way of the leak (no attempt is made to stop or fix the leak) and in so doing notices that there is a wedding invitation under the sofa that never got mailed. The closest thing he has to a cabinet meeting is a voice mail from his father, who's locked himself out of his hotel room and doesn't know what to do.

FOUR HOURS BEFORE THE WEDDING

The groom's day gets more enjoyable when he goes out to lunch with his groomsmen. Even though everyone will be having an enormous four-course dinner in a few hours (that costs $250 per person), the groomsmen decide to take you out for chili burgers and cheese fries. You stand up to give a mini-toast and tell the groomsmen how much they mean to you personally, but suddenly double over from intestinal pain.

The bride, meanwhile, is testing the capacity of the bridal suite. In addition to her earlier cabinet, she's now added a hairdresser, a makeup person, the entire staff of the hotel, and every female on the guest list. The temperature in the room is approaching 120 degrees. The bride suddenly snaps. She orders everyone out of the room. They oblige, and twenty seconds later the bride is unsure why she did that, so she asks everyone to come back in.

ONE HOUR BEFORE THE WEDDING

As the bride is putting on her dress, she notices that one of the decorative beads sewn to the dress is missing. She then begins sobbing and makes all the women in the room—including her ninety-two-year-old grandmother—get down on their knees and start looking for the bead.

Meanwhile, in the groom's hotel room, the best man's full house beats the groom's three of a kind.

FOUR MINUTES BEFORE THE WEDDING

The best man, standing beside the groom, tells the groom that if he wants to bail, just say the word and they'll be in a car heading for Mexico. The groom thanks the best man for his kind offer but says he's feeling surprisingly calm. The best man asks again, pointing out that Mexico is really pretty this time of year and he'd love to see it. Eventually, the best man just leaves and goes to Mexico on his own.

At the same moment, the bride is outside the venue, stepping out of a limo that costs about five thousand dollars to rent. The bride's mom starts to cry and tells her baby girl that she's a beautiful angel. The bride's dad reiterates that he doesn't think the groom is good enough for his baby girl. And down the aisle they go!

Part 2: The Ceremony

The bride and groom's days merge. They are thrilled to have finally reached this moment, but the excitement is just beginning.

TWO MINUTES INTO THE CEREMONY

It's the groomsmen's moment to enter. Despite pleas from the wedding planner to go slow, the groomsmen walk down the aisle at a pace befitting a Kenyan marathoner.

The bridesmaids, on the other hand, walk so slowly you wonder if they're being paid by the minute. The reason for the molasseslike pace? Even the most humble and generous bridesmaid will be a little upset that this day isn't about her, so she makes her seventeen seconds of fame last as long as she can.

FOUR MINUTES INTO THE CEREMONY

The bride is about to walk down the aisle. The musicians start playing "When the Saints Go Marching In," even though this is not the song your bride had selected. The bride and the planner stare at each other in awkward horror, before the planner says, "Kid—start marching." Making matters worse, the father of the bride loves "When the Saints Go Marching In," so he does some sort of improvised Cajun jig.

SEVEN MINUTES INTO THE CEREMONY

The officiant lights a few candles, to symbolize the eternal love that the bride and groom feel for each other. When he returns the candles to their holders, however, one of them isn't inserted securely. The burning candle begins to list to one side, like the Leaning Tower of Pisa. Everyone in the place—including the bride and groom—is transfixed by the leaning candle. Will it tumble over and set the place on fire? Is that a bad omen for the bride and groom's eternal love?

The officiant has his back to the candle, though, and sees none of this. Eventually, one of the groomsmen steps forward and straightens the candle, much to everyone's relief.

TWENTY MINUTES INTO THE CEREMONY

The bride and groom have the ceremonial drinking of the wine. The crowd holds its breath when the bride takes a sip, nervous that she'll spill red wine on her dress. She doesn't, and no one seems to care when, moments later, the groom splatters wine all over his new tux.

THIRTY-FIVE MINUTES INTO THE CEREMONY

The officiant asks if anyone knows of a reason why the bride and groom should not be married. Several people stand up, but the bride and groom have already told the officiant to ignore these people and go ahead with the marriage.

FIFTY MINUTES INTO THE CEREMONY

People start heading for the reception, even though the ceremony isn't over yet.

ONE HOUR INTO THE CEREMONY

The officiant pronounces the couple husband and wife. The groom kisses the bride, one moron yells, "Slip her some tongue!" and you're married!

Part 3: The Reception

You and your bride are suddenly completely euphoric. The hard part is over—now's it time to celebrate! Not that celebrating doesn't also have its difficulties:

ONE MINUTE AFTER THE CEREMONY ENDS

The bride and groom ask for five minutes alone together before the pictures start being taken. Their request is denied.

SEVEN MINUTES AFTER THE CEREMONY ENDS

The photographer has hired a math Ph.D. from Harvard to calculate every possible family-member permutation that can be captured in a picture. Even though she's already shot four hundred exposures, she still needs to get a shot of the bride with the groom's uncle, the groom's boss, the wedding planner, and a St. Bernard.

THIRTY MINUTES INTO THE COCKTAIL HOUR

Martial law is declared at the savory crepe station.

FORTY-FIVE MINUTES INTO THE COCKTAIL HOUR

The caterer officially runs out of red wine and vodka, both of which were supposed to last another five hours. Disgruntled, the guests start lining up at the entrance to the ballroom, even though the staff is still setting up.

ONE HOUR INTO THE COCKTAIL HOUR

The guests finally breach the ballroom doors and the reception begins. The bandleader announces the arrival of the bride and groom, but none of the guests seems to notice because they are all still trying to find their tables.

FOUR MINUTES INTO THE RECEPTION

The bride and groom have their first dance. Despite spending five hundred dollars on dance lessons, you both instantly forget all the steps that you've spent weeks learning.

ONE HOUR INTO THE RECEPTION

While the guests eat dinner, the bride and groom start making the rounds to say hello to everyone. The guests are somewhat annoyed that they have to stop eating and talk to the bride and groom, especially because the majority of people at the reception have never met the bride and groom before.

AN HOUR AND A HALF INTO THE RECEPTION

The best man gives his toast, which is basically a summary of all the "hilarious" toasts that people gave at the rehearsal dinner. This makes everyone who wasn't at the rehearsal dinner feel sufficiently awkward and left out.

TWO HOURS INTO THE RECEPTION

Some guy who's not a particularly good dancer makes everyone on the dance floor gather around him in a big circle while he attempts to break-dance.

TWO HOURS AND TEN MINUTES INTO THE RECEPTION

The photographer finally finishes taking family portraits. Did she miss anything important during the five hours she was away?

TWO AND A HALF HOURS INTO THE RECEPTION

The band has officially played all their good covers. They begin a medley of some of their original compositions. Cue the cake cutting!

TWO HOURS AND FORTY-FIVE MINUTES INTO THE RECEPTION

Your guests have officially reached the we've-eaten-the-cake-now-can-we-get-the-hell-out-of-here moment.

THREE HOURS INTO THE RECEPTION

The venue manager tells you that you've reached the time limit. You can keep the party going for another half hour if you want to pay five hundred dollars for the space and three hundred dollars for the band. It takes you three seconds to declare that the reception has ended.

Part 4: The Wedding Night

You and your new wife are both completely exhausted. But before you can go to bed . . .

THIRTY MINUTES AFTER THE RECEPTION ENDS

A party has broken out in the bridal suite because all your friends needed some place to hang out. The caterer had sent some food and champagne up for the bride and groom to enjoy, and it's quickly consumed by your sister's boyfriend.

AN HOUR AFTER THE RECEPTION ENDS

You finally get everyone out of the bridal suite by lying and telling them there is free booze in the lobby. You lock the door once they leave and ignore the knocks and drunken shouts that hound you until dawn because there is still some important business at hand. You and your bride need to consummate your love with some husband-and-wife sex. You turn down the lights, slip under the covers... and immediately fall asleep.

Knock Her Socks Off

Congratulations, my friend! You've done it! You've truly knocked your bride's socks off by becoming her husband. You've given her the two things she's ever really wanted in life: a wonderful companion and a large store credit at Williams-Sonoma.

For the Bride

Ladies, you must admit: Your guy didn't do half bad, did he? Yes, he knocked one of the centerpieces over and made the photographer get a picture of him doing armpit farts, but who cares? He put a lot of effort into being a great groom and passed with flying colors. You should be proud.

One of the best ways to ensure that you can both remember the high you're on during the wedding is by sharing one of those corny thoughts that will be in your head for much of the night. At some point, lean over and tell your new husband what you're thinking, whether it's "This is amazing" or "I love you so much" or "Is that your uncle vomiting in the corner?" The memories will last forever...

21

Warning! Don't Ask These Questions!

While this book attempts to answer many of the big questions that the average groom will likely have during his engagement, there are still some questions that are off-limits and should *not* be asked. These questions tend to fall into one of five categories.

CATEGORY 1: QUESTIONS THAT ARE TOO STUPID, EVEN FOR A MAN

Your bride will cut you a lot of slack when it comes to asking dumb questions about the wedding. She's aware that in asking questions you're showing interest in the planning and trying to learn more. However, it's nice to enter the marriage without your new wife thinking you're a total moron. To that end, think twice before you ask the following questions, because you can probably figure out the answers on your own:

- Where do the centerpieces go?

- When are we getting back our nonrefundable deposit?

- Our invitations need a sixty-cent stamp. Where do I get those?

- Why do all the envelopes for the reply cards have the same address printed on the front of them?

- When's the Sunday brunch?

CATEGORY 2: QUESTIONS THAT HAVE NO ANSWER

A lot of guys have difficulty understanding that there are questions out there that simply don't have answers. This is true of both existentialism (What is the meaning of life?) and wedding planning. Continually asking your bride questions about the wedding planning that have no answers will only serve to frustrate both of you. So don't ask them. And if you mess up and do ask them, don't follow up your unanswerable question with another unanswerable question like, Well, why isn't there an answer?

- Should we be having more fun?

- Why is everything so complicated?

- Should I be feeling so stressed out?

- Are we making good decisions?

- Is this what other people's wedding-planning experiences are like?

- Why are you upset with me?

CATEGORY 3: QUESTIONS THAT HAVE ALREADY BEEN ASKED AND ANSWERED

This is a favorite category for most guys. We ask a legitimate question, get an answer, and then ask the same question again, sometimes mere minutes later. Why? Either we're stupid (possible) or we're so surprised about the answer that we ask the question again to passive-aggressively show our displeasure (likely). It's better to express your concerns openly and honestly. Or, better yet, not at all.

- Are all these flowers really necessary?

- Do I have to do what the planner says?

- Is anyone really going to notice the hand calligraphy on the invitations?

- Why are you going in for another dress fitting if you just had one yesterday?

- Why can't I walk down the aisle to "I Want Your Sex"?

CATEGORY 4: QUESTIONS THAT HAVE NOTHING TO DO WITH WEDDING PLANNING

There are certain moments when your bride will be in the middle of intense planning—she's at the cake place, talking to her mom on the cell phone while putting stamps on the envelopes and writing her vows—and the last thing she needs to hear is some random-ass, non sequitur question from you, such as:

- Should we have Indian food tonight?

- Do you think I should get this mole on my arm looked at?

- Does that lamp in the bedroom take a sixty-watt bulb or a hundred-watt bulb?

- Is eleven a prime number?

- Who said, "Don't fire until you see the whites of their eyes"?

- Do avocados have good cholesterol or bad cholesterol?

CATEGORY 5: QUESTIONS THAT MAKE YOUR FIANCÉE FEEL LIKE A HOOKER

These are the most dangerous questions of all:

- If I come to the florist with you, can we have sex tonight?

- On our honeymoon, can we stay at a hotel that rents rooms by the hour?

- I'll put on my tux...but will you take it off?

- Why send the videographer home at midnight?

Keep in mind that some questions can fit into more than one category. For example: Don't you think I look like George Clooney when I put on my tux? is a question that's both stupid and has already been asked and answered.

While, Babe, did you have a lesbian fling in college? manages to (a) ask a non sequitur, (b) make your bride feel like a hooker, and (c) once again ask a question that's already been asked and answered. Job well done!

Obviously, all the questions listed in this chapter are merely examples. There are many other terrible and inappropriate questions that you can come up with if you put your mind to it. Best of luck.

22

Reward Yourself Using This Checklist

Everyone deserves a little treat after working hard on a project. When the sea lion at the aquarium jumps through a hoop, he gets a fish. Sadly, enclosing a fish in this book was deemed unsanitary, so instead here's a checklist of some little ways in which you can reward yourself after you've mastered the lessons in each chapter.

**Check Here When
Task Is Complete**

Chapter 1
Having sufficiently understood
the similarities between bridal
magazines and porn magazines,
take one last sentimental look

Check Here When
Task Is Complete

through your supply of porn before
throwing it all away. From now on,
the only magazine in your house
with pictures of naked people
should be *National Geographic*.

Chapter 2
Having agreed to hire The Dictator wedding planner, allow yourself five minutes (and only five
minutes) to daydream about doing
the seating chart with J. Lo, had
you been able to hire her.

Chapter 3
Having successfully beaten out
The Other Couple for the wedding
venue, have a glass of champagne
and celebrate. (Note: While this is
happening, a third couple will
probably swoop in and steal the
venue from you.)

Chapter 4
Having successfully registered for
your china, you are now allowed to
break one of your old plates to get

**Check Here When
Task Is Complete**

the clumsiness out of your system.
Also, it helps clear shelf space.

Chapter 5
Having found all of the vendors
you are going to use, go to an ATM
and get one last receipt showing
your prewedding checking account
balance. Frame this receipt and put
it in your den with a caption that
reads: The Good Old Days.

Chapter 6
Having finalized the guest list,
spend one last evening with the
friends who aren't on it, before
they stop speaking to you.

Chapter 7
Having successfully ordered your
cake, go to your favorite bakery
and splurge on an item you've always wanted to try but thought
was overpriced. Discover that a
seven-dollar cookie seems totally
reasonable now that you've bought
a thousand-dollar cake.

**Check Here When
Task Is Complete**

Chapter 8
Having successfully chosen your
groomsmen, spend a few minutes
reflecting on how much each of
them means to you as a friend (except for the three dudes in the
bridal party whom you've never
met before).

Chapter 9
Having survived the first hunting
trip with your future father-in-law,
spring for the expense of either a
great psychiatrist or a bulletproof
vest. At least one of them will be
useful if you have to go hunting
again.

Chapter 10
Having finally mailed your wedding invitations, treat yourself to a
relaxing massage. It will be the last
few moments of peace you enjoy
before you realize you forgot to include the reply cards.

**Check Here When
Task Is Complete**

Chapter 11

Having successfully put together
an activity packet for your out-of-
town guests, e-mail all your local
friends and brag about how you've
managed to make a Denny's and a
park bench sound as exciting as the
Eiffel Tower.

Chapter 12

Having survived your most recent
meltdown about an inconsequen-
tial wedding-planning detail ("I
can't believe we're serving Atlantic
salmon and not Pacific salmon!"),
go clear your head by attending a
baseball game with a buddy. It'll
feel great to be outside, having a
dog and a beer...until you nervously look around the stadium
and think, This is how many people are coming to the wedding.
Another meltdown soon follows.

**Check Here When
Task Is Complete**

Chapter 13
Having successfully taken your
wedding band off your finger (at
last!), take a few minutes to admire
how pretty the ring is. This will
help distract you from the fact that
your finger is now bright red and
numb from the ring-removal process.

Chapter 14
Having finally selected the dinner
menu for the wedding reception,
go and have a TV dinner by yourself, just so you can remember
what it's like to eat without conflict.

Chapter 15
Having gotten your tuxedo for the
wedding, spend a few minutes ad-
miring how good you look in it.
Now turn your cummerbund
around; it's upside down.

**Check Here When
Task Is Complete**

Chapter 16
Having successfully written your
own vows, refer to yourself as
Shakespeare for a few days—until
your fiancée's laughter becomes
unbearable.

Chapter 17
Having made it home from your
bachelor party in one piece, have a
nice lunch with your fiancée ... because after the Nevada state police
catch up with you, you won't be
seeing her for a while.

Chapter 18
Having successfully made your
honeymoon plans, buy a fun travel
magazine, which will help get you
in the mood for your big trip. Of
course, the place you're going on
the honeymoon looks nothing like
the place in the magazine, but
your fiancée doesn't need to know
that. Yet.

**Check Here When
Task Is Complete**

Chapter 19
Having survived the barrage of
awkward toasts, reward yourself by
going home and taking a look at
the seating chart for the following
night. Did someone bring up your
ex-girlfriend even though you told
him not to? Looks like he's suddenly sitting at Table 109.

Chapter 20
You did it! You're married! Give
your new wife a big hug and a kiss,
because she loves you despite the
fact that you snore, spill potato
chips on the floor, and still haven't
fixed the screen door that you accidentally walked into last summer.

Conclusion
It's All Worth It

No matter how many disasters, fights, and flesh wounds occur during the engagement and on the wedding day, you won't remember any of them. Not a one! And, amazingly, neither will anyone else. If a fire breaks out during your ceremony, people will remember that the wedding was "warm and cozy." If people get food poisoning at the reception, everyone will remember the "exotic cuisine."

So why do we make modern wedding planning so complicated if it's all going to turn out okay in the end? The answer, as is so often the case in life, can be found in the wisdom of *The Karate Kid*. It's the classic wax on–wax off scenario. You're unknowingly building skills that you'll be glad you have later in life. If you can get through your wedding planning and make it to the big day, not only will you be rewarded with a great celebration and a wonderful spouse, but you'll also be able to solve all the problems that you'll encounter along the road of life.

Life Problem	Solution Learned at Wedding
Your kids are fighting about who gets to sit in the front seat of the car.	You invoke the diplomatic skills you learned while listening to your family argue about who would get to sit in the front row at the wedding: "If you keep fighting, everyone will sit in the back!"
You spill red wine on your new carpet.	The trick is salt and seltzer, which the waiter taught you at your reception after he spilled red wine on the bride's dress.
It's your mom's birthday and you forgot to get her a present.	Anything can be regifted. Looks like mom's getting a crystal dish!
The roof in your new home is leaking.	You know a great contractor because your sister brought him as a date to your wedding under the premise that they were madly in love and going to get married. (They broke up four days later.)
Aliens land in your backyard and start attacking.	You take them out using the assault rifle your crazy uncle Ned got you as an engagement gift.

Certainly, some of the stuff you've learned may never come in handy. I know what a votive, an aisle runner, and a

Chivari chair are, but doubt that knowledge will be of much use to me—although you never know. I may open up a votive store someday. Stay tuned.

But I can say, unquestionably, that it's all worth it in the end, because you're in love. And there's absolutely nothing in the world that's better than being in love.

Except maybe Doritos.

Acknowledgments

For their help, guidance, and frequent laughter at the jokes in this book, I would like to thank the following people: my agent and friend, Jennifer Joel; my editor at Bloomsbury, Panio Gianopoulos; Francesca Delbanco and Nick Stoller, who gave me some valuable notes when I was putting together the book proposal; Katie Sigelman, who, among other things, is always so friendly on the phone; Lisa Gorjestani, who helped my wife and me plan our wonderful wedding while patiently answering all of the 793 questions that I had along the way (for the record, she's the nicest person in the world and *not* a dictator); my parents, Bill and Ronnie Scott; my "new" parents, Vicki Fox and Larry and Paulette Fox; and all the members of my incredibly supportive family (both the family that I've had forever and the one into which I've recently married).

Most especially, I'd like to thank my wife, Emily, who not only agreed to marry me, thus making this book possible, but is also the most talented writer that I know.

A Note on the Author

A graduate of Harvard University, Peter Scott has written for both television and film. He hopes to have children someday so that he can take another intimate and important moment in his life and turn it into a funny book. He lives in Los Angeles with his wife.